BERLITZ

HONG KONG

1988/1989 Edition

Zhu Hai   *29 Promces*
            5 Aut. Regni
            西藏 Tibet

Beijing
Shanghai   *4 Special Economic*
Canton   *Bones.*

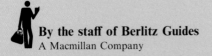

By the staff of Berlitz Guides
A Macmillan Company

14th Printing

How to use our guide

- All the practical information, hints and tips that you will need before and during the trip start on page 103.

- For general background, see the sections The Territory and the People, p. 6, and A Brief History, p. 16.

- All the sights to see are listed between pages 24 and 54. Our own choice of sights most highly recommended is pinpointed by the Berlitz traveller symbol. Special sections on Macau and Guangzhou (Canton) with their own practical information summaries are to be found between pages 55 and 73.

- Entertainment, nightlife and all other leisure activities are described between pages 74 and 91, while information on restaurants and cuisine is to be found on pages 92 to 102.

- Finally, there is an index at the back of the book, pp. 126–128.

Text: Ken Bernstein
Photography: Walter Imber
Layout: Doris Haldemann
Cartography: ⬤ Falk-Verlag, Hamburg.

Contents

The Territory and the People

Hong Kong wraps up all the excitement, mystery, glamour and clamour of the Orient—without the inconvenience.

Lavish home comforts ease the visitor's culture shock amidst junks and sampans, black pyjamas and coolie hats, chopsticks and joss sticks.

Packed into skyscrapers and double-deck trams and buses, the people of Hong Kong—98 per cent are Chinese—work hard and live fast, making the

most of imperialism's last hurrah in this hotbed of capitalism and commerce.

The only thing you might miss is solitude, in short supply in the over-populated metropolis. To get away from it all, you can take a bus to the hinterland, where water buffalo still do the drudgery. Or sail to a deserted isle; Hong Kong has a couple of hundred to spare.

Of the territory's 236 islands, the one called Hong Kong ("Fragrant Harbour") is best

For all its bilingual capitalistic bustle, Hong Kong and its people retain their profound Chineseness.

known and contains a quarter of the total population. Yet it accounts for only a small fraction of the colony's real estate, most of which is on the Chinese mainland in the so-called New Territories. The British leased this land from China at the end of the 19th century. The contract expires at midnight, June 30, 1997, whereupon Hong Kong will become a Special Administrative Region of the People's Republic of China.

Traditionally, Hong Kong's role was that of a trading post; now, the economy has moved into the booming realm of manufacturing and exports. Local factories sell textiles, clothing, toys, electronics and plastics to the world. The work force, taking home Asia's second-highest wages, is highly motivated. So are the bosses, who pay only 16½ per cent business profits tax.

The laissez-faire economic scene attracts investors from all sides, not least from China itself. The territory has long been China's handiest window on the West. This is only one of the reasons behind Beijing's (Peking's) announced determination to maintain Hong Kong's prosperity and stability.

According to a 1984 agreement between the Chinese and the British, Hong Kong will remain a capitalist enclave after the People's Republic takes control in 1997. The Hong Kong dollar, the currency of the world's third biggest financial centre, will remain freely convertible. And Hong Kong people are assured representative government, continued free speech and travel, and justice based on British law.

The territory's exact area is a flexible figure, growing slightly from year to year as land is reclaimed from the sea. It's just above 400 square miles—in the same league as Tahiti, Martinique or the Orkneys. But more than five million people are crammed into the islands, and the population density is duly noted in the record books.

Thanks to the subtropical climate, the people can escape from their sardine-can living quarters into the streets. Thus the round-the-clock drama of bargain-hawkers, noodle-vendors, hair-cutters, bone-setters, fortune-tellers and story-tellers. The sights and sounds make priceless memories.

Tens of thousands of people

Trying to beat the housing crisis, boat people by the thousand park their homes in Aberdeen harbour.

8

beat the housing problem as part of the floating population. In Hong Kong the term is literal: they live on junks in harbours and typhoon shelters, three or four generations with their pet birds and dogs. Thousands more squat in squalid shack communities. At the other extreme of society, Chinese millionaires affect luxuries as conspicuous as ocean-view mansions and lucky-number licence plates (that cost a fortune at government auctions) on their fleets of limousines.

Hong Kong has hundreds of Christian churches and chapels but the great majority of the population tends to Buddhism, Taoism or Confucianism. Chinese holidays, solemn or riotous, are eagerly observed. In temples crammed into narrow streets, or monasteries aloof in the wilderness, a multitude of gods are worshipped.

One way or another, fate and luck are usually on the mind in Hong Kong. Astrologers and fortune-tellers do a steady business. On a higher level, before a skyscraper is built for example, a *fung shui* (wind and water) investigation approves its site, and the spirits must be placated. Gambling is a passion: cards, mah-jong, the lottery, the horses. Hong Kong supports

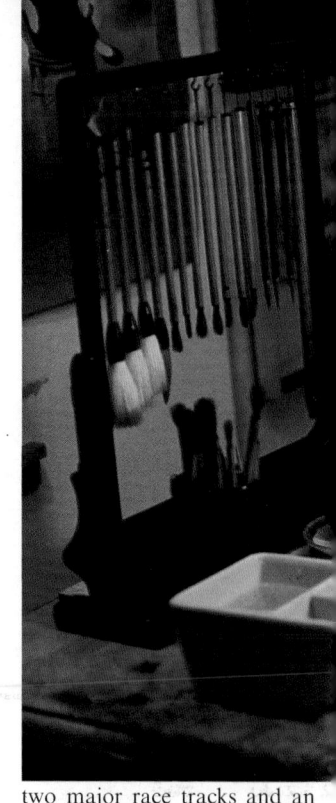

two major race tracks and an intensive off-track betting system.

The people of Hong Kong are good at numbers; watch an abacus in a race against an electronic calculator. They're also good at letters, the 26 of the English language. Even in an isolated village you'll find

Calligrapher at work: words he paints are beautiful enough to frame.

someone who can muster a few words of English. The population is highly literate: over one hundred Chinese-language newspapers are published in Hong Kong (four English dailies, as well). Most people in Hong Kong speak Cantonese, a dialect unintelligible to natives of Beijing or Shanghai. But the **11**

A Kowtow to Chinese

Chinese is the world's No. 1 language—native to more people than any other. It has written the history and culture of a nation for thousands of years.

Each character represents an idea, not a sound, and how it's written means a lot to the Chinese, who consider calligraphy a serious art form. Writing a single character requires from one to 33 pen or brush strokes. Chinese can be written from left to right or from top to bottom, or in some cases from right to left.

The spoken language has additional challenges. The dialects in various regions can be as different as English and French. The Cantonese spoken in Hong Kong is difficult for foreigners because it uses up to seven different musical inflections—"tones"—to distinguish otherwise identical syllables.

written language is the same everywhere.

Sightseeing in Hong Kong starts at sea level with a harbour as big and perfect as San Francisco's or Rio de Janeiro's. The traffic is enthralling—a bubbling cosmopolitan stew of freighters, ferries, hydrofoils, tugs, junks, sampans and yachts. See it from a ferryboat weaving through the nautical throng, or look down on it all from Victoria Peak. At 1,800 feet the Peak is a modest enough mountain, but it's the island's summit in altitude and social standing as well.

Elsewhere on the island, the sights match every interest and mood. Be serious among the commercial skyscrapers in this great centre of Asian finance. Or escape to Tiger Balm Garden, an oriental ancestor of Disneyland, or the new and novel Ocean Park to look at the fish, animals, birds and views. Curiosity—or just an appetite for seafood—might lead you to Aberdeen, the liveliest fishing harbour you've ever seen. And you need no excuse to investigate the island's dozen principal beaches.

Across Victoria harbour is the mainland, starting in the overcrowded Kowloon peninsula with its hotels, nightlife and almost non-stop shopping. Beyond, in the New Territories, the colony changes character from mile to mile: here a brand-new suburb, there an industrial complex, beyond that a wilderness of fish ponds, duck farms and banana plantations. Near the frontier, the terrain becomes as pastoral as the China of old water-colours. You can climb to the lookout point at Lok Ma Chau and peer out over no man's land and the Chinese "special economic zone" (SEZ) beyond.

Nowadays you don't have to be satisfied with a glance through binoculars at the People's Republic of China. The Beijing government is welcoming foreign tourists in ever more significant numbers, and Hong Kong is the principal gateway. You can sign up for a tour of Guangzhou (Canton) and the surrounding southern sights by jet plane or hydrofoil or the venerable railway.

The most popular getaway spot for the people of Hong Kong is the Portuguese enclave of Macau, less than an hour's ride by jetfoil. The 400-year-old blend of Iberian and Oriental cultures makes this a fascinating place, full of old colonial grace and boundless Chinese energy and ingenuity. With its cobbled streets and sandy beaches, Macau can be calm and restful. The other side of the coin, or chip, is a revel of roulette, blackjack, fan-tan, dog-racing and jai-alai—enough to exhaust any go-go gambler.

Back in Hong Kong, you'll need time and strength—and money—for the shopping. The range of choice is exciting. But to find exactly what you want at the best price requires concentrated comparison shopping. The bargains are as old as traditional Chinese porcelain and as new as the latest cameras and hi-fi rigs.

Another area in which Hong Kong excels is food. You'll never be disappointed, whether you're smothered in luxury in one of the top restaurants or munching a morsel bought from a pushcart. This is the place to try every kind of Chinese cooking, not only the familiar Cantonese but specialities from lesser-known gastronomical regions. And when you yearn for more commonplace flavours, Hong Kong is well endowed with European restaurants of almost all persuasions; even hamburger joints and pizza parlours, if you insist.

Nightlife is not as one-sided as you may have been led to believe by the garish neon signs. Yes, there are a thousand Suzie Wongs in Wanchai and Tsim Sha Tsui. But Hong Kong also has sophisticated cabarets, arts festivals, and its own philharmonic orchestra.

The wail of Chinese opera, the clang of a tram, the chant of a pedlar, the clatter of mahjong tiles: Hong Kong is never still. It's as dynamic, and unpredictable, as a typhoon.

13

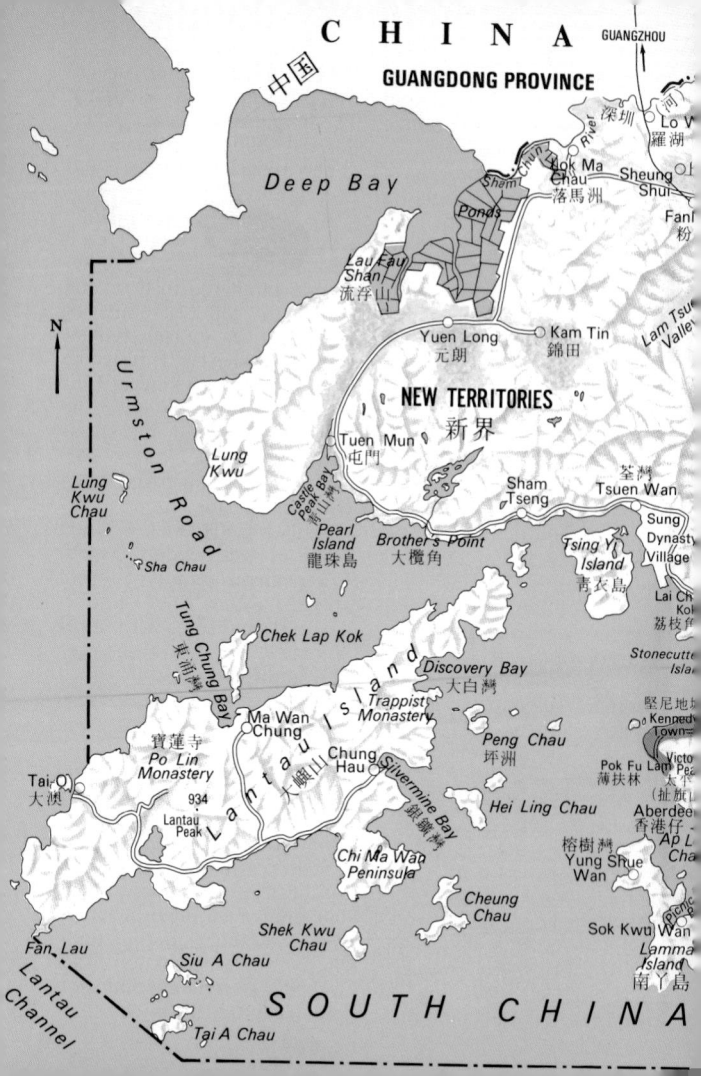

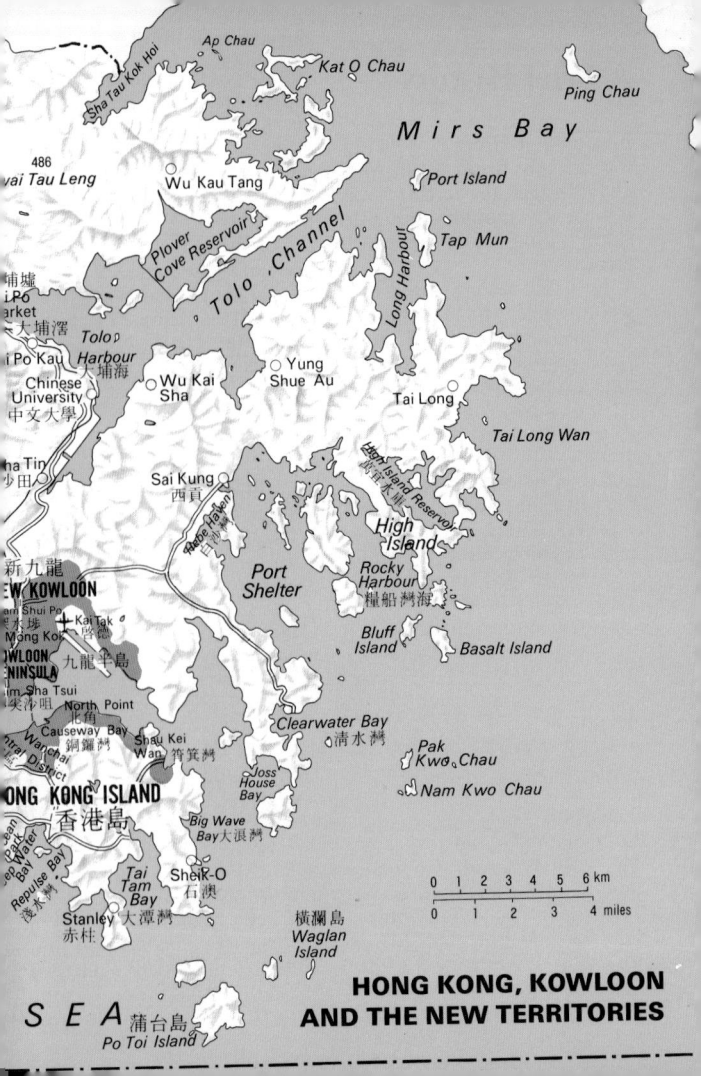

A Brief History

Accounts of Hong Kong's history usually begin in the year 1841. In fact, the territory was populated—though insignificantly—long before the British arrived.

For the record, fishermen were settled on Lamma and Lantau islands several thousands of years ago. Later, during Europe's Middle Ages, the port of Shek Pai Wan (now called Aberdeen) flourished as a pirates' lair. In the New Territories, Chinese settlers lived their lives in traditional walled villages; otherwise little happened. Hong Kong was still underdeveloped in the mid-19th century when Lord Palmerston dismissed it as "a barren island with hardly a house upon it". The Foreign Secretary thought the place had no future. He was not only grumpy, he was monstrously mistaken.

The China Trade

Long before Palmerston's days, the British East India Company had established a thriving business in Canton, buying Chinese tea, silk and porcelain for an insatiable English market. But trading conditions were difficult. The Chinese emperor considered his country both self-sufficient and superior. He also kept the traders confined to a ghetto area to minimize the harmful influence the "foreign devils" might exert on the population in general.

For the British the problem was not so much one of dignity as of a simple balance of payments crisis. China would accept nothing but silver bullion in exchange for its goods. Britain had to find a more abundant commodity to square the accounts—something other than silver to fill the holds of the clipper ships on the way to the East.

Around the turn of the 19th century the traders found the answer: opium. They loaded it in India and delivered it to Canton. China outlawed the trade in 1799, but local Cantonese officials were always willing to look the other way for a consideration, or "squeeze money", as it is still known in Hong Kong. The traffic in opium became so intense that China's silver surplus began to melt away.

The Manchu emperor finally laid down the law in 1839. He assigned Commissioner Lin Tse-hsu to go to Canton and stamp out the smuggling of opium—"foreign mud", as the Chinese called it. Bribable bureaucrats panicked at Lin's appointment; his incorruptibility was notorious.

Lin's crackdown was severe. He demanded that the British merchants in Canton surrender all their opium stores. To back up the ultimatum he laid siege to the traders, confined as they were to their Canton quarters. After six tense weeks the top British official on the scene, Captain Charles Elliot, promised the merchants compensation if they would obey Lin. They surrendered over 20,000 chests of opium to the commissioner and retreated to temporary sanctuary, first in Macau, later on ships anchored in Hong Kong harbour.

A year later, in June 1840, a British naval force was dispatched to retaliate against the Chinese, thus beginning the first of the so-called Opium Wars. After a few skirmishes and much negotiation a peace agreement was established. Under the Convention of Chuenpi, Britain was given the island of Hong Kong and on January 26, 1841, Elliot proclaimed it a British colony.

At lighting-up time, Hong Kong traditionalist puffs bamboo pipe.

Opium War II

The peace plan drafted at Chuenpi was short-lived. Both Peking and London repudiated the agreement. Fighting resumed. This time the British forces—less than 3,000 strong but with superior weapons and tactics—outfought the Chinese. Shanghai fell and Nanking was threatened, so the Manchus were forced back to the negotiating table. In the Treaty of Nanking (1842) China was compelled to open five of its ports to foreign economic and political penetration, and even to compensate the opium smugglers for their losses. Hong Kong's status as a British colony and a free port was confirmed.

In the aftermath of the Opium Wars the trade in "foreign mud" was resumed at a level even higher than before, although the major traders—by now respectable and diversified—stopped it in 1907. The British didn't abolish opium smoking in Hong Kong until 1946; in China the new Communist government followed suit in 1949.

Thriving Colony

The man who won the Opium War and the peace that followed, Sir Henry Pottinger, became the first governor of Hong Kong. Under his enthusiastic direction the colony began its march toward what he predicted would be "a vast emporium of commerce and wealth".

And he was right. Almost as soon as the Union Jack was hoisted, Hong Kong's population and economy began to grow steadily. One surprise was the sizeable number of Chinese who chose to move to the colony in spite of its unfamiliar rules and rulers. One early governor, Sir John Francis Davis, fed up with the squabbling of the English residents, said, "It is a much easier task to govern the 20,000 Chinese inhabitants of the colony than the few hundreds of English".

Despite the differences between the Chinese majority and the European minority, relations were generally cordial except during one rare incident. On January 15, 1857, somebody added a secret ingredient to the dough at the colony's principal bakery: arsenic. While the Chinese were enjoying their daily rice, the occidentals, eating their daily bread, were dropping like flies. Many Europeans became seriously ill, including the governor's wife. At the height of the panic engendered by the poison plot, thousands of Chinese were deported from Hong Kong, but

Hong Kong Glossary

Getting around is difficult when place-names are pronounced totally differently in English and Cantonese. To give you a headstart, here are 15 troublemakers: in the first column, the customary English name, in the second column, the approximate Cantonese pronunciation. And if that fails, point to the Chinese characters in the third column.

Aberdeen	Heung gong jai	香港仔
Causeway Bay	Tung lo wan	銅鑼灣
Central district	Jung wan	中環
Cross Harbour Tunnel	Hoi dai sui do	海底隧道
Happy Valley	Pau ma dei	跑馬地
Mandarin Hotel	Man wa jau dim	文華酒店
Ocean Park	Hoi yeung gung yuen	海洋公園
The Peak	San deng	山頂
Peak Tram	Lam che	纜車
Peninsula Hotel	Boon do jau dim	半島酒店
Post office	Yau jing guk	郵政局
Railway station	Fo che jam	火車站
Repulse Bay	Chin sui wan	淺水灣
Stanley	Chek chue	赤柱
Star Ferry Pier	Tin sing ma tau	天星碼頭

no one ever discovered the identity, or was ever certain about the motives of the culprit or plotters.

By a treaty in 1860 Britain gained a permanent beachhead on the Chinese mainland—the Kowloon peninsula, directly across Victoria harbour from Hong Kong island. In 1898, under the Convention of Peking, China leased the New Territories and 235 more islands to Britain for what then seemed an eternity—99 years. But as the deadline neared, China reiterated its repudiation of the "unequal" treaties and vowed to recover sovereignty, triggering tremors of uncertainty in Hong Kong and beyond.

Twentieth Century

Hong Kong's laissez-faire economy was ideal for the exploitation of modern technology. In 1903 the China Light and Power Company was generating electricity; a year later trams rattled along their new waterfront tracks. Soon wealthy colonists were importing cars to take advantage of **19** the few miles of newly paved roads.

In 1912 the governor, Sir Francis Henry May, and his wife were being carried in sedan chairs from Blake Pier when a would-be assassin fired point blank. The shot was as wild as the gunman. The bullet splintered the frame of Lady May's sedan chair but no one was injured. It was the only violence ever aimed at a Hong Kong governor.

The colony's population fluctuated according to events beyond its borders. In 1911, when the Chinese revolution overthrew the Manchu Dynasty, refugees flocked to Hong Kong. Hundreds of thousands more arrived in the 1930s when Japan invaded China. By the eve of World War II, the population was more than 1½ million, far more than could be housed.

A few hours after Japan's attack on the American fleet at Pearl Harbour in December 1941, a dozen Japanese battalions began an assault on Hong Kong. The colony's inadequate defences were caught unready. Five minutes of bombing destroyed Hong Kong's minimal air force on the airfield at Kai Tak. Abandoning the New Territories and Kowloon, the defenders retreated to Hong

Typhoon

Whatever the derivation of the word—some say Chinese, others Arabic or Greek—no natural danger is more of a threat to Hong Kong than a typhoon.

With modern techniques of surveillance and early warning, precautions can be taken. Nevertheless these severe tropical cyclones with winds of 75 miles per hour and more can —and do—cause casualties and damage almost every year.

Sometimes though, the elements outdo themselves; such was the case in 1873. When the blow was over, up to 3,000 people were dead or missing, hundreds of local junks and sampans had been lost, as well as 35 foreign ships and the roof of the governor's "typhoon-proof" bungalow.

But the worst was yet to come. In 1906 the killer-typhoon of all time struck the colony, taking perhaps 10,000 lives. Some 40,000 boat people were left homeless after the devastating storm which, concentrated on the Kowloon peninsula, was over in less than two hours.

Going places: rickshaw and Union Jack on governor's limousine are reminders of colony's history.

Young scholars in bilingual school learn simple Chinese characters.

Kong island, hoping for relief which never came. They finally surrendered on Christmas day, 1941. Veterans recall three and a half cruel years of hunger and concentration camp existence. The occupation forces deported many Hong Kong Chinese to the mainland, so the population was down to half a million by the time of Japan's defeat in 1945. At the end of World War II, Hong Kong took stock of the remains—no industry, no fishing fleet, and few houses or public services for the survivors.

Postwar Growth

China's civil war sent distressing echoes to Hong Kong. As the Chinese Communist armies gained the upper hand over the Nationalists and drove towards the south, the flow of refugees calamity spurred the government to launch a crash programme of public housing construction. The new spartan blocks of flats, grimly overcrowded, soon put cheap and fireproof roofs over hundreds of thousands of heads.

But even a frenzy of construction couldn't keep pace with the demand for living space. Refugees continued to flee China, legally and illegally. In 1962 the colonial authorities reluctantly closed the border to turn back the overwhelming tide. Chinese who crawled, swam or sailed to Hong Kong risked arrest and deportation back to the People's Republic. The number of legal immigrants—the ones with exit visas issued by Beijing—is still so high that Hong Kong is hard pressed to meet the demand for housing and services.

into Hong Kong multiplied. Soon after Canton fell and the People's Republic was proclaimed, the population statistics (1950) showed that Hong Kong now numbered two million people. Housing was desperately short.

The problem became an outright disaster on Christmas Day, 1953. An uncontrollable fire devoured a whole "city" of squatter's shacks in Kowloon; 50,000 refugees were deprived of even primitive shelter. The

On the positive side, the millions who chose a new life brought their energy, ambition and skills to Hong Kong. They opened the way for a new economic boom: Hong Kong's traditional role of trading middleman has been eclipsed by its potential as an industrial and financial centre. Back-alley workshops and advanced electronics factories are exporting Hong Kong's new reputation to all the world. **23**

What to See

Kai Tak airport and most of Hong Kong's hotels are in Kowloon*, on the mainland side of the territory. The crowded Kowloon peninsula and the booming but often bucolic New Territories call for some serious sightseeing. But for orientation, we begin across Victoria Harbour on Hong Kong island, where the colony was founded. The island remains the capital of government and commerce, and a compact cross-section of all the territory's delights and pungent contrasts.

Hong Kong Central

No matter how many tunnels and transit systems may speed cross-harbour traffic, nothing matches the excitement of the **Star Ferry** between Kowloon and Hong Kong. Bells ring, Chinese deck-hands in blue sailor suits man the hawsers, and a couple of hundred commuters begin a seven-minute adventure. As the big green-and-white boat weaves through an ever-changing obstacle course of large and small craft, the soaring **skyline** of Hong Kong Central draws closer. If the captain fails to make a

Upper-class yachts and humblest houseboats share Causeway Bay shelter in sight of famed skyline.

three-point landing, passengers mill about impatiently until the gangplank bangs down and everyone rushes ashore. (Travellers in a hurry know that second-class, on the bottom deck, not only costs less but is faster: fewer steps from ship to street.)

Outside the terminal, tourists are solicited by rickshaw drivers as ancient as their vehicles. Many visitors as well as local residents are indignant to see one man pulling another in a carriage. If your conscience prevents you from taking a ride, you can settle for a posed photograph in the passenger seat. The driver, always ready to smile for a camera, will demand a model's fee.

Just west of the ferry terminal is Hong Kong's modern General Post Office, with the Government Publication Centre on the ground floor.

* Kowloon, meaning Nine Dragons, is pronounced more or less the same in English and Cantonese. But English place-names are usually unrecognizably changed in Cantonese. The brief glossary on page 19 may help when asking directions. Or point to your destination on our maps.

24

Drop in for free Tourist Association brochures and maps. You can also buy more substantial books on local history, economy and sociology, along with wall-sized maps and charts.

More maps and publications are available at the headquarters of the Hong Kong Tourist Association, on the 35th floor of the Connaught Centre. Brightly-uniformed specialists are on hand to answer your questions in any of several languages. The 52-storey Connaught Centre, a striking grey building with porthole-shaped windows, cannot fail to catch your eye.

In Hong Kong, **City Hall** is not the place to look for politicians or bureaucrats. They're dispersed in office buildings in various parts of town. City Hall is, instead, a modern cultural centre occupying 100,000 square feet of

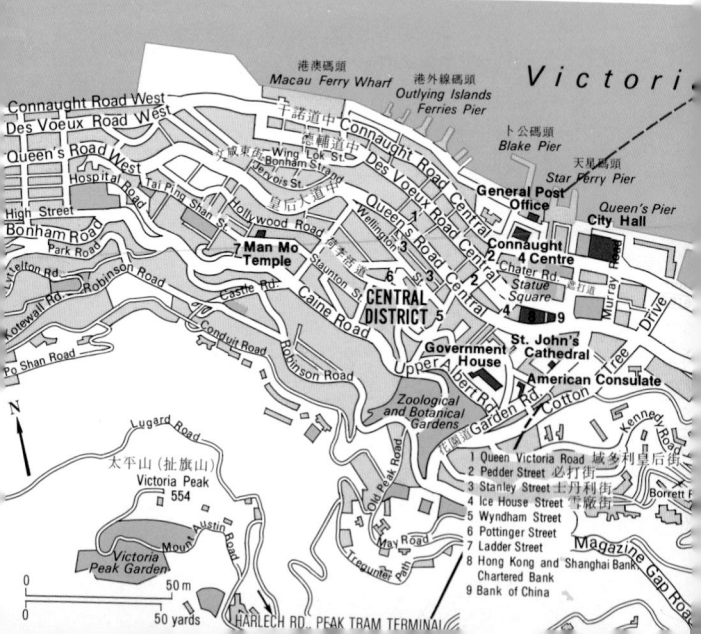

Crash Programme

Be quick, if you want to see Hong Kong's colonial glories: they're tumbling down like a pack of cards. Victims: the 1879 Hong Kong Club, the Hong Kong and Shanghai Bank and the Repulse Bay Hotel... Despite spirited attempts to save the buildings from the bulldozers, so short is the colony of suitable land to develop that there is little that can be done. Government monument-preservation policies require payment of huge compensation. Thus by 1990 most of Hong Kong's colonial history will probably have vanished. Of the 70-odd buildings belonging to this category listed in 1976, nearly a quarter have already gone, and the others crouch under the threat—even the Anglican Cathedral.

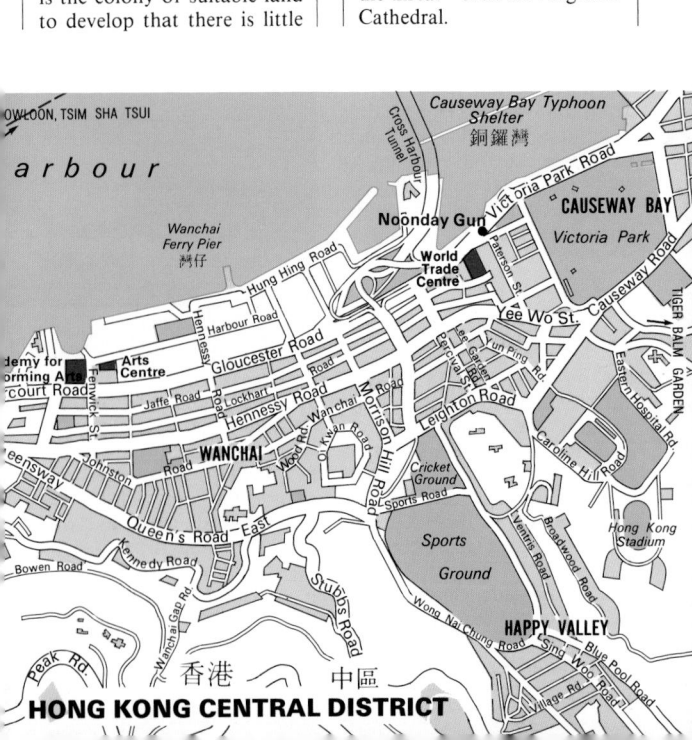

HONG KONG CENTRAL DISTRICT

prime harbour-side land just east of Star Ferry. Among the facilities are the Hong Kong Museum of Art (see p. 85), a library and a 1,500-seat concert hall.

The whole district, except for Statue Square and Chater Garden, is characterized by the frenzied construction of new skyscrapers. But notice one timeless detail: no matter how tall the building under construction, the scaffolding is always bamboo, not metal. It's much lighter, and it works.

All the trams in Hong Kong pass along **Des Voeux Road.** So does most of the money, as you'll realize when you see the rows of vital financial institutions.

To the Summit

For more than 90 years the most exhilarating way up to Victoria Peak has been by funicular. The **Peak Tram** starts across the street from the American Consulate in Garden Road and climbs, in some places at a startlingly steep incline, to 1,305 feet. The right-of-way slices alongside fancy apartment blocks, bamboo stands and jungle flowers. Passengers **28** crane their necks for dizzy-ing glimpses of the harbour.

Originally steam-powered, the Peak Tram was built to speed commuters to the mountainside residential areas. This was long before the automobile age. Sedan chairs and rickshaws, the only alternatives, were slow and expensive. Since the tram's inauguration in 1888 it has only stopped for typhoons and World War II.

The 80-passenger cars make the journey in eight minutes. On fine Saturdays and Sundays

Street-corner fortune-teller reads between the lines of client's palm.

you may have to brave a crowd queueing up at the lower terminal. During the spring and autumn festivals, when Chinese traditionally seek out the hilltops, the throngs are so large you would be better advised to try another time; buses and taxis are packed.

At the funicular's upper terminus there's a restaurant and shopping complex resembling an airport control tower. Indeed, you can look down on the planes taking off and—more exciting—landing at Kai Tak while you stop for coffee or a meal. From here you can walk 360 degrees around the peak in 45 minutes. Lugard Road and Harlech Road have benches for a rest and a **view** of the Hong Kong coastline and many an island.

If you're up to a climb, take Mount Austin road to the Victoria Peak Gardens. They used to belong to the governor's mountain lodge, but the building was demolished by the Japanese during the occupation of Hong Kong.

Back to the lower terminal of the Peak Tram it's a short walk to the governor's official residence, Government House, which also suffered in World War II. The Japanese rebuilt it according to their own taste in palaces, creating an uneasy compromise between Oriental and colonial style. From the outside it still looks like a potentate's folly, but the interior has been restored to western imperial grandeur.

Across Upper Albert Road from the mansion, the **Zoological and Botanical Gardens** provide an oasis amidst the big-city pressures. In the very early morning the park is taken over by deadly-serious shadow-boxers doing *tai-chi* exercises. These fitness enthusiasts, young and old, go through ballet-style movements in slow motion to discipline mind and body. The park has a modest zoo. See the monkeys, jaguars, mountain lions, peacocks, storks, pink flamingoes and weird and wonderful chattering jungle birds.

More City Sights

Man Mo Temple is the island's oldest house of worship, though the date of its founding is subject to dispute. Visiting firemen may feel homesick for the firehouse when they walk into the pall of smoke from all the burning joss sticks and the incense coils hanging from the ceiling. The gold-plated sedan chairs on the left side are for carrying statues of the temple's gods around the neighbourhood on holidays. The statues, visible in the main shrine, represent Man and Mo, notable for intellectual and military prowess.

The temple faces Hollywood Road, a street otherwise known for its shopping. The windows and open doors of the shops reveal an alluring range of oriental antiques—furniture, carpets, carvings, porcelain and bronze, ivory and jade. Elsewhere along Hollywood Road the shops are even more serious; they sell coffins, wreaths and burial wear. The area is known as Cat Street Centre.

Intersecting Hollywood Road, the aptly named Ladder Street is a pleasure to walk—downhill. The incline is too steep for vehicles, so the roadway consists of stone steps. Local residents used to be borne up the street in sedan chairs.

Less than half a mile away another popular stair-street also intersects Hollywood Road. This is Pottinger Street, lined with busy shops and stalls mainly devoted to household goods.

When the lights go on in **Wanchai**—a five-minute tram ride from the financial district—you don't have to read Chinese to know what they're selling. Neon scare-headlines shriek "Bar", "Nightclub" and "Topless" in Chinese, English and Japanese. Men on the loose are personally invited into the cool, dark establishments by doormen in flamboyant costumes or by lounging, leering ladies. The beer, as advertised, is cheap but not the drinks for which the companionable girls thirst. Servicemen relaxing from the rigours of the Vietnam

Hong Kong woman attends to her devotions at the Man Mo temple.

war poured millions of dollars into the Wanchai boom of the 1960s. Now office towers are replacing many of the old sinful premises.

There is, however, an attraction for all here at the Museum of Chinese Historical Relics (see p. 85). The glass and steel **Academy for the Performing Arts,** at the western end of Harbour Road, also draws the crowds.

Causeway Bay, about a mile east of Wanchai, has become a prosperous tourist district with the construction of giant new hotels and a mass of good restaurants. Heavy traffic on the waterfront highway divides the two personalities of the neighbourhood. On the nautical side is the Causeway Bay **typhoon shelter.** Here the rich-man-poor-man contrasts of Hong Kong glare: the yachts are anchored almost gunwale to gunwale with the overcrowded houseboats of the fishermen.

Just opposite the World Trade Centre, the **Noonday Gun** lives up to its name every midday. The tradition dates back more than a century. According to the legend, Jardine, Matheson & Co., the pioneer Hong Kong *hong* (trading company), fired a private salute for a visiting tycoon. This incensed the colonial authorities, who claimed the sole right to issue 21-gun welcomes. The merchants contritely agreed to limit the salvoes to one a day—signalling the noon hour for all, and for ever.

On the landward side of Causeway Bay, a hectic commercial life goes on far into the evening. Aside from important Hong Kong, Japanese and Chinese department stores, the area has hundreds of small shops selling clothing, food and household goods. When restaurant, cinema and shopping crowds all converge, the pedestrian traffic slows to a cheerful crawl amidst food carts, fortune tellers, and hawkers flaunting towels, toys and trinkets.

Farther inland, a branch line of the tram system loops around one more district of metropolitan Hong Kong: **Happy Valley.** The name stirs mixed emotions. At one time it was a miserable valley, a swampland conducive only to breeding malarial mosquitos. Then the terrain was assigned to the development of the colony's first racetrack. Hong Kong gamblers are so avid to play the horses that Happy Valley is still thriving, even after the opening of a bigger and

Itinerant chef offers snacks to Hong Kong's floating population.

Take a Tram

People in a hurry take a taxi, a bus, a minibus or the MTR. But hundreds of thousands of travellers take a tram every day. It happens to be fun.

The ancient trolley-car system is the most leisurely and revealing way to see Hong Kong. With more than 20 miles of track, the jerky double-deckers cover almost the entire north coast of the island.

Try to get a seat on the upper deck for the best views of Hong Kong: jammed flats, rice stalls, tea shops, temples, pushcart vendors, coffin makers, umbrella factories, tape-recording counterfeiters, Chinese checker competitions...

The western terminus is in Kennedy Town, an overcrowded city in itself, named after a 19th-century Hong Kong governor, Sir Arthur Kennedy. The eastern extremity, Shau Kei Wan, once a pirates' hangout, still has a colony of "boat people" who live on junks and sampans parked in the bay.

When the trams were first brought to the colony they symbolized the breathtaking technological future that awaited it. Now, with the patina of venerability unmistakably upon them, they are the very stuff "old" Hong Kong is made of, as much as the junks in the harbour.

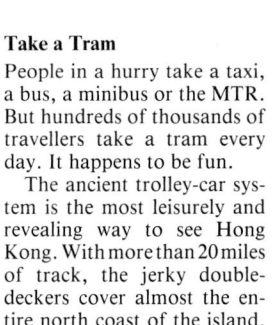

better track on the mainland at Sha Tin.

In the Happy Valley area you'll also find the eccentric **Tiger Balm Garden.** It was founded in 1935 by the late Aw Boon Haw, who became a millionaire by producing a medicine called Tiger Balm. (It is not made from tigers, but it does promise to cure colds, headaches, rheumatism, gout, toothache, scorpion bites and many other problems.) With its garish pagodas and statuary, the garden is an obvious setting for souvenir photos.

Round the Coast

Aberdeen, the island's oldest settlement, has the largest "floating population"—thousands of people who spend their entire lives on junks and sampans in the **harbour.** It makes for a blaze of local colour: barefoot children frolicking on the poop deck, housewives hanging up the laundry or playing mah-jong, elderly folk watching the sunset, dogs and cats underfoot, songbirds in bamboo cages overhead … and all afloat.

There are water taxis galore, including small sampans with women drivers; they propel the craft by hand, like gondoliers. You will be proposed a sampan tour of the choked port. For a less extensive excursion you can take the new fly-over across to the island of Ap Lei Chau, redolent of fresh wood from scores of junks and sailboats under construction in local boatyards.

For years Aberdeen's floating restaurants have been a tourist attraction. The raw materials are impressive; if you can't make it to the pre-dawn auction at the vast local wholesale **fish market,** have a look at the retail street market later in the day. The fish are still flipping fresh.

Near the bus terminal is a temple built by local fishermen in 1851. It is dedicated to Tin Hau, the Queen of Heaven and Patroness of Seafarers. Originally the temple was on the shore but reclamation projects have left it high and dry. On the 23rd day of the Third Moon the birthday of the Taoist goddess is celebrated here and in all Hong Kong fishing communities.

The peninsula opposite the east coast of Ap Lei Chau island has been developed into a site containing Ocean Park and Water World. **Ocean Park**

Ap Lei Chau boatyard awash in lumber for junks and sailboats.

has become one of Hong Kong's greatest attractions. The Oceanarium, said to be the largest in the world, features displays by performing dolphins, killer whales, seals and pelicans. An enormous roller-coaster, way above the sea, space wheels, high-diving shows and the longest outdoor escalator in the world guarantee a day of excitement. Linking the lowland and highland sections of the park, a cable-car system offers spectacular views across to the islands of the South China Sea.

A sandy beach leads to **Water World,** a large-wave pool connecting up with many others. Five giant spaghetti-like slides wind down the hillside, while an inner-tube rapids ride, jacuzzi and water cannon complete the scene. Fast-food kiosks and a Chinese restaurant ensure that you will not go hungry. Water World is open from April to December.

Continuing anti-clockwise round the coast, Deep Water Bay has a good beach and an enviable flotilla of resident sailboats and yachts. The next inlet is more famous: **Repulse Bay.** The roomy, sandy crescent,

Coolie-hatted fishwife weighs the catch at Aberdeen street market.

backed by green hills, is so attractive and so easy to reach that it is packed with sunbathers all summer long.

Stanley was one of the main fishing villages on Hong Kong Island. Today it has grown into a market town and is a popular residential area. The market is a mecca for bargain hunters, selling overrun designer jeans and clothes in Western sizes as well as rattan furniture, brassware and porcelain.

Kowloon

Though much smaller than Hong Kong island, Kowloon has almost twice the population. In many streets the density reaches the equivalent of 150,000 inhabitants per square kilometre, an appalling crunch of humanity overflowing onto the tenement roofs.

Most of Kowloon's attractions for visitors are centred near the tip of the peninsula in the district known as **Tsim Sha**

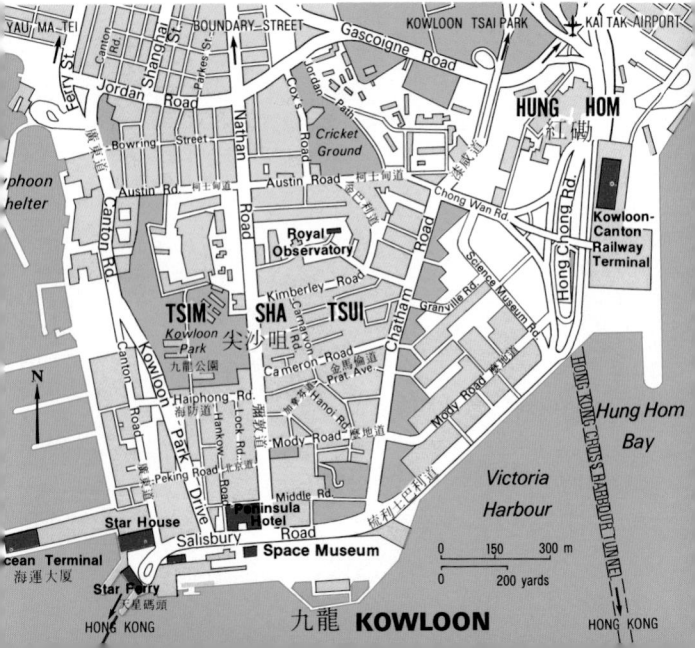

Tsui. Near the Star Ferry terminal the dust has been flying in a frenzy of redevelopment of the waterfront district. This is where you'll find the Hong Kong Space Museum, with its futuristic architecture. In an unusual conservationist move, the historic (early 20th-century) clock tower of the original Kowloon-Canton Railway terminal has been spared from demolition. The terminal itself was torn down after being replaced by a new one about a mile away in Hung Hom, a grand and spacious station by any standard, but more so in relation to the number of trains arriving there. It is often the scene of emotional family reunions as legal immigrants arrive from China.

Part of the new station complex is the even newer Hong Kong Coliseum, called the largest indoor and air-conditioned auditorium in all Asia. It seats 12,500 sports or music fans.

The most exciting view of the Kowloon peninsula is the one from an airplane coming in to land at Kai Tak airport. The final approach passes so low over the rooftops that passengers can see the laundry hanging out like flags on bamboo poles jutting from every room. The runway is more than two miles long, so landings are not the heart-stopping dramas of yore. The airport expansion was achieved by reclaiming land from the sea.

In another reclamation project, more than 150 acres of new land became Tsim Sha Tsui East, a vital commercial district. Luxurious hotels are found in TST East along with multi-storey shopping plazas and office buildings. And a waterfront promenade provides a sublime view of Hong Kong across the harbour.

Kowloon shops lure with luxuries. Bird-lovers, opposite, take tea.

Kowloon's main street, **Nathan Road,** was created when Sir Matthew Nathan was Governor of Hong Kong (1904 to 1907). At the time, many thought it absurd to build a tree-lined boulevard through what was almost wilderness. Now the former "Nathan's Folly" is called the "Golden Mile". The glittering hotels, restaurants, night-clubs and shops attract constant crowds.

A shopping phenomenon, Kowloon's **jade market,** happens every day from about 10 a.m. to 4 p.m., in the Yau Ma Tei district of Nathan Road, beneath the fly-over. Vendors of jade, a stone which has had special meaning to the Chinese for centuries, squat on shoebox-sized benches, spreading their rings, brooches, beads and figurines over the pavement.

In North Kowloon (in Lai Chi Kok Road) a relatively new sight is the **Sung Dynasty Village.** This is a beautifully designed full-sized model village reproducing the houses, shops, temples and gardens of the era of the Sung emperors (960–1279). Traditional Chinese artists and artisans show how they work; historical personages fill a wax museum; and Chinese food is celebrated as well.

New Territories

Hong Kong's New Territories, "borrowed" from China until 1997, begin at Boundary Street. Surprises are everywhere: new industrial complexes alongside languorous farming villages, skyscraper towns blooming in the middle of nowhere, women in coolie hats tending water buffalo, and flashes of azalea. Ask at the tourist authority about tours from Kowloon.

The highway makes a circuit of the New Territories, beginning with the new town of TSUEN WAN, in an area of heavy industry just west of Kowloon. The population is more than half a million and destined nearly to double before the building project is completed. The route continues parallel to the coast. A single 9-mile stretch of shore here accounts for one-third of all Hong Kong's beaches. Places are often referred to in terms of the nearest mile-post, measured from the tip of the Kowloon peninsula. Thus "19½-mile beach" is at Castle Peak Bay.

At the 21 milestone, near the huge new town of TUEN MUN,

Barely half an hour's drive from Kowloon's bright lights, old farm life survives in New Territories.

is a Taoist retreat called **Ching Chung Koon.** This spacious modern complex contains temples and pavilions, statues and gardens. It is known for its collection of bonsai (miniature plants). Among the ponds is one inhabited by turtles. Visitors toss in coins in hopes of bouncing one off a turtle's head—a sure way of achieving good fortune.

The main road continues clockwise round the New Territories to the big market town of YUEN LONG (site of a boisterous trade in live ducks). A side road goes to the coastal village of Lau Fau Shan on Deep Bay.

Wild and Beautiful

Remote areas of the New Territories are happy sighting grounds for bird-watchers. Hundreds of species have been recorded, from everyday egrets and funny-faced cockatoos to mynahs and pelicans.

As civilization encroaches, wild animals have been vanishing: leopards haven't been seen in the New Territories in 20 years. But you can still come across barking deer, monkeys, porcupines and scaly anteaters. In the wilderness you may also stumble upon a banded krait, a cobra, or some other fearsome snake. Though sightings are common, bitings are rare.

Crops in New Territories depend on intensive toil, as reflected in lined face of an old Hakka woman.

The townsfolk work oyster beds which supply Hong Kong with fresh shellfish and export markets with dried oysters and oyster sauce. In the village restaurants they know all manner of recipes for preparing the local delicacy; but don't eat them raw.

Much of the area from Yuen Long to the Chinese border is given over to fish-ponds and duck-ponds, a moody scene that seems to belong to a China of long ago. Another image right out of Chinese history is the walled village of **Kat Hing Wai*** a couple of miles east of Yuen Long. It's built in a square, and the only way in is through the gate in the brick defensive wall—where tourists are invited to make a contribution "for the welfare of the village". Kat Hing Wai was built four or five centuries ago by the Hakka people, who had migrated from North China. You see Hakkas throughout the New Territories; the women are identifiable by their flat straw hats with black "curtains" hanging round the rim. Ladies in black pyjamas sit

---

* Also known as Kam Tin.

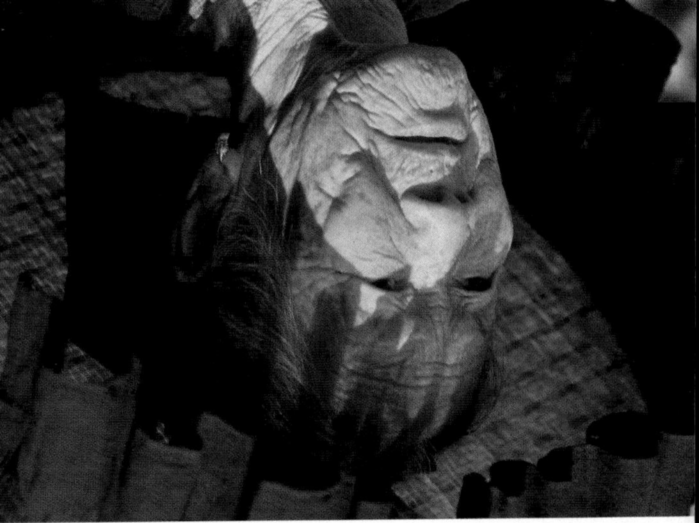

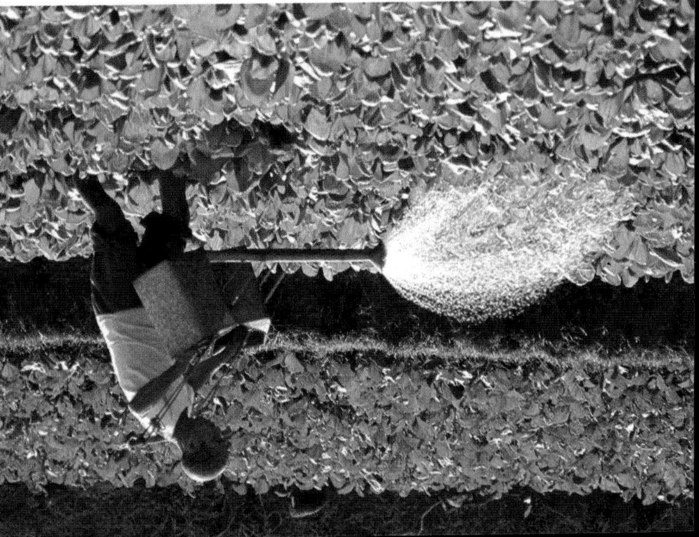

around the entrance to the Kat Hing Wai compound playing cards, occasionally dropping out to tend one of the souvenir stalls. Incidentally, in this old village everyone belongs to the same clan, so they all have the same surname, Tang. All the Tangs know who's who.

Lok Ma Chau is Hong Kong's "window on China"— the place from which you can gaze across the Shum Chun River into the daily life of villagers in Guangdong Province.

In the years of China's isolation from the West, tourists would go to the Lok Ma Chau lookout point to rent

binoculars for a glimpse of the great mystery beyond. Now that China has embraced foreign tourism, though, much of the drama has dissipated. But the bird-watching is still exciting.

A tightly patrolled "prohibited zone" prevents unauthorized Chinese from getting anywhere near the river bank. Illegal immigrants, intent on swimming to Hong Kong, usually come by sea, over great distances fraught with danger.

Though the railway goes right to the border at Lo Wu, travellers who lack visas can only go as far as the station at SHEUNG SHUI. Heading back to Kowloon, the highway and railway stay close together from FANLING, the site of the best golf courses in the country.

The railway line curves gracefully alongside **Tolo Harbour,** an idyllic body of water well protected from the open sea. You can take a ferryboat through the harbour, past the ingenious **Plover Cove** reservoir. This 40,000 million gallon water catchment area was appropriated from the sea by damming and draining a broad inlet. The boats go on to the friendly fishermen's island of TAP MUN, in Mirs Bay, with stops in various remote hamlets of the unspoiled **Sai Kung peninsula.** On the south side of the peninsula are some of the territory's best beaches.

From the next railway station, University, you can see

Kowloon-Canton train rumbles by Tolo harbour. Hillside buildings belong to the Chinese University. **47**

Thirsty Territory

Those huge black pipes you see here and there in the New Territories are pumping Chinese water to the Hong Kong waterworks. Fresh water from Guangdong Province, purified on the Hong Kong side of the border, accounts for about one-quarter of the territory's entire supply.

All the ingenious, multi-billion-dollar reservoirs, plus a costly desalination plant, can't guarantee that the supply will always equal the demand. In times of drought Hong Kong has to curtail the hours when consumers may turn on the tap.

the modern campus of the Chinese University of Hong Kong. Unlike the older, British-style University of Hong Kong (at Pokfulam on Hong Kong island), the Chinese University uses both Chinese and English for teaching. You don't have to be a student to rent one of the rowing boats moored here to sample the pleasures of Tolo Harbour.

At SHA TIN the Monastery of 10,000 Buddhas looks down on a burgeoning new town. You have to walk up hundreds of stone steps in the hillside to reach **Man Fat Temple,** with its regiments of small gilt statues of Buddha lining the walls. In-

defatigable climbers will want to go up to the top of the nine-storey pink pagoda for a panoramic view.

The newest attraction in Sha Tin is the **racecourse** opened in 1978 at a cost of more than 500 million Hong Kong dollars. Every touch of luxury has been thought of—including air-conditioned stables and a nine foot deep swimming pool for the horses. (Swimming is a good conditioning exercise for racehorses as well as human athletes.)

Two natural rock formations are always pointed out on excursions. Sha Tin Rock, more often called **Amah rock,** is a pile of several rocks which resemble a woman with a baby in a sling on her back. A legend says a local woman climbed the hill every day watching for her husband to return from across the sea; one day the wife and her child were turned to stone, a permanent symbol of her faith and longing.

Closer to town is **Lion Rock,** shaped like a lion lying in wait. It's one of those rare rock formations that really look the part; the tourists know its name before the guide can translate it.

Schoolgirl meditates before one of Buddha statues at Sha Tin.

Islands

Excursion companies sell various orientation cruises of Hong Kong harbour including a look at some outlying islands. These pleasant but expensive outings can lay the foundation for your own explorations aboard the cheap, usually comfortable ferries used by the islanders themselves. From the ferry terminals on the overpopulated north coast of Hong Kong island you can escape to islands without cars or cares, where the natives smile "hello" and point you toward a secret beach.

Lantau Island

The biggest island in the colony, Lantau, covers nearly twice the area of Hong Kong island, but its population totals only about 30,000. All those wide open spaces barely 6 miles east of Hong Kong explains the rush of city folk to Lantau on weekends and holidays.

At 3,064 feet, Lantau Peak is high enough to attract the odd passing raincloud—and refreshingly cool breezes on most hot summer days. The biggest community on the island, **Tai-O,** lives from fishing, rice-farming and duck-breeding. Many of the inhabitants live, one way or another, on the water—either aboard houseboats or in houses on stilts in the main creek.

Ferryboats from Hong Kong go to three Lantau ports, the closest at Silvermine Bay on the east coast. The village of SILVERMINE BAY, with its sagging old drawbridge across the inlet and incongruous new eight-storey buildings, doesn't quite come up to picture postcard standards. Nearby DISCOVERY BAY, an up-and-coming resort area, proves more attractive.

A bus service, badly overstretched on weekends and holidays, links Silvermine Bay with Lantau's famous Buddhist monastery. The road passes pastures, miles of beaches and picnic areas galore, then climbs steep, scenic hillsides to reach **Po Lin monastery**. In spite of all the tourists, the setting is peaceful. Grey-robed monks with shaved heads float past picnickers (warned by signs in Chinese and English not to bring any meat on to these vegetarian premises). The big, modern Buddhist hall is only one of several shrines at Po Lin.

The hillsides near the monastery are the site of Hong Kong's only tea plantation. Visitors are welcome to enter the 60-acre establishment, watch how tea is processed, and taste the end product.

You can visit another **mon-**

astery, this one housing Christian monks, on a hillside overlooking the east coast of Lantau. It is reached in three stages: a commuter ferry from Hong Kong to PENG CHAU (a small island just off Lantau); the monastery's shuttle ferry from there; and a 15-minute uphill walk from the jetty to the monastery. The Trappists, who fled Peking during the Chinese civil war, have been on Lantau since their monastery was completed in 1956.

Hikers enjoy the two-hour cross-country trek from the monastery down to Silvermine Bay. But the authorities warn: be on the lookout for snakes, which can be plentiful in the Lantau hinterland, especially in summer. *Hints:* Carry a stick; if you encounter a snake stand still; never attack a snake, but wait for it to go away.

Ferry glides across "main street" of Lantau island village, Tai-O.

Cheung Chau

This small island of about 40,000 people, mostly fishermen, has had a chequered past in the smuggling and piracy business. That era has gone now, but other elements of the simple old life are nicely preserved. They still carve jade, paint silk and build junks—all by hand. They still hang out the fish (heads discreetly wrapped in paper) to dry in the sun. Hence the **waterfront** sometimes smells like an Eskimo village, but no one minds, not even the business-suited expatriates who have settled on the island and commute by ferry to their offices in noisy, high-rent Hong Kong.

Cheung Chau becomes the centre of Hong Kong life once a year, usually in May, during the Bun festival, a folklore extravaganza (see Festivals, p. 86). The rest of the year, life goes on at its accustomed pace: rickety machines chugging in two-man factories, children in

A stitch in time at ornate shrine of Po Lin monastery on Lantau.

spotless school uniforms being ferried home to houseboats, retired fishermen stirring smelly shrimp paste, dogs of the most improbably mixed breeds sleeping in the pathways.

By way of formal tourist attractions, **Pak Tai temple** has some fine carvings and a great iron sword said to be 600 years old. The temple, built in 1783, is dedicated to a Taoist sea divinity credited with rescuing the villagers from a plague. Pak Tai temple is only a short walk from the ferry landing. The island has several other temples and shrines as well. On the less serious side, Cheung Chau has good beaches and, of course, plenty of fresh seafood.

Lamma Island

Only a couple of miles off the south-west coast of Hong Kong island, Lamma is a handy getaway island for swimming, hiking, picnicking, birdwatching… or just sitting back to watch the bananas grow.

Life on Lamma, if not totally primitive, gets close to the essentials. There are no cars, not even motorbikes, and the few bicycles have nowhere much to go. The area is less than one-fifth the size of Hong Kong island, and none of the villages have more than a few hundred inhabitants. Archaeological traces indicate that Lamma was inhabited some 4,000 years ago; the island is known somewhat glamorously as "Hong Kong's Stone Age Island".

Modern ferryboats from the Hong Kong Government Pier East Wing go either to **Yung Shue Wan,** the principal settlement of Lamma's north-west, or **Sok Kwu Wan,** on the east 53 coast. Either village has good waterfront restaurants with home-style Chinese food, principally seafood fresh from the tank. Both ports are within hiking distance of beautiful beaches.

You can return to the modern world aboard the creaky old ferry to Aberdeen. The crossing is brief but stimulating, as transistorized picnickers from the big city mingle with islanders whose baggage runs from oil drums and free-roaming chickens to caged snakes.

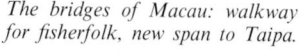

The bridges of Macau: walkway for fisherfolk, new span to Taipa.

Excursions

⚑ Macau

The last bastion of Portugal's great 16th-century empire, Macau is more than just a historical quirk. Here, where East and West first met, life is as colourful as a Chinese dragon but as relaxed as a siesta in the sun.

Under the circumstances, the incongruous becomes routine: the latest jetfoil skimming past traditional junks; a Chinese temple alongside a Portuguese fortress; computerized betting on an ancient ball game; trucks and buses with twin licence

plates—black and white from Macau, yellow and black from China.

For years the Portuguese foothold has been as delicate as an egret's status on the back of a rhinoceros. China is 600,000 times bigger than Macau. In recent times the 6 square miles of Macau and its two offshore islands has been officially termed a Chinese territory under Portuguese administration. But all that history is to end in 1999, when the enclave reverts to direct Chinese rule.

Macau's population is estimated at 450,000; an appallingly high figure for such a small area. Yet the visitor feels little of the sardine-tin complex of Hong Kong, 40 miles away, where there sometimes seems no room to breathe. The traffic jams in Macau, mercifully, are still 10 years behind the rest of the world. A trace of tropical lethargy adds to the charm in a city of outdoor cafés, palm trees, pedicabs, peeling pink and green buildings and blind fortune-tellers under the arcades. But the torpor definitely ends once inside the doors of Macau's casinos, scene of some of the liveliest gambling west of Las Vegas.

The story of Macau began in 1513 when a Portuguese explorer, Jorge Alvares, reached the south coast of China. Traders soon followed, setting up bases in several parts of the Pearl River estuary. Eventually, in 1557, they were all consolidated in Macau. It was Europe's only gateway to China; through Macau flowed western technology and religion. In 1576 Pope Gregory XIII created the Macau diocese, covering all of China and Japan. No less impressive were the secular challenges. China and Japan weren't on speaking terms, so trade between them had to be channelled through a neutral middleman. Lucky Macau exactly fit the specifications.

Portugal's near-monopoly of East-West trade understandably fanned the competitive instincts of other European powers. The most unrestrained reaction came from the Dutch, who sent an invasion flotilla to Macau in 1622. The defenders triumphed.

Still, the golden age was dimming. As China relaxed its trade restrictions, Macau's significance dwindled. The lonely Portuguese outpost was rarely heard from.

One of the most poignant eras for Macau was World War II, when Portugal's neutrality assured the territory a flood of refugees and a swarm of spies

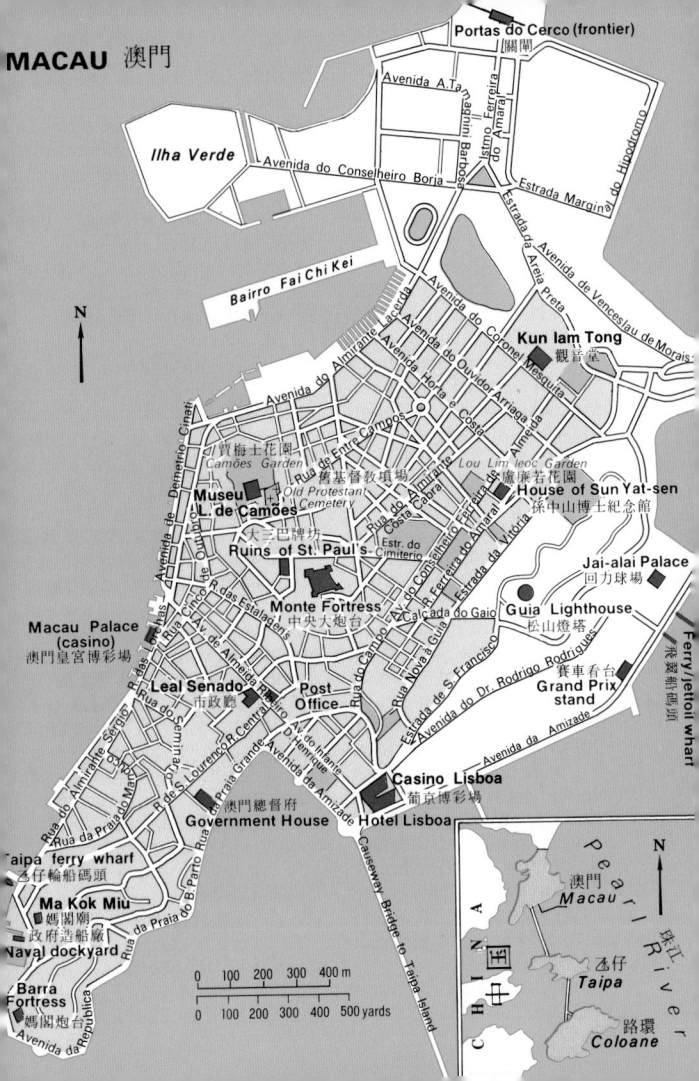

MACAU 澳門

Portas do Cerco (frontier)
關閘

Ilha Verde

Avenida A.T.amagnini Barbosa

Avenida do Conselheiro Boria

Estrada Margin

Estrada da Areia Preta

Istmo Ferreira do Amaral

Avenida de Venceslau de Morais

Bairro Fai Chi Kei

Avenida do Coronel Mesquita

Kun Iam Tong
觀音堂

N

Avenida do Almirante Lacerda

Avenida do Ouvidor Arriaga

Avenida Horta

Rua de Entre Campos

Avenida do Coronel

Camões Garden
白鴿巢賈梅士花園

Lou Lim Ieoc Garden
盧廉若花園

Museu
L. de Camões

Old Protestant
Cemetery
舊基督教墳場

House of Sun Yat-sen
孫中山博士紀念館

天三巴牌坊

Ruins of St. Paul's

Estr. do
Cimiterio

Jai-alai Palace
回力球場

Demetrio Cinati

Rua do Almirante

Avenida Conselheiro Ferreira de Almeida

Avenida da Praia

Rua Formosa

Calçaba Gabra

Monte Fortress
中央大炮台

Macau Palace
(casino)
澳門皇宮博彩場

Guia Lighthouse
松山燈塔

Calçada do Gaio

Rua das Estalagens

Avenida da Sidónio Pais

Leal Senado
市政廳

Estrada de S. Francisco

Estrada da Vitoria

Avenida Nova à Guia

Grand Prix
stand
賽車看台

Ferry/jetfoil wharf
飛翼船碼頭

Post
Office

Rua Central

Avenida do Dr. Rodrigo Rodrigues

Avenida da Amizade

Rua da Praça Grande

Avenida da Amizade

Casino Lisboa
葡京彩場

Rua do Almirante Sergio

Rua de S. Lourenço

Government House
澳門總督府

Hotel Lisboa

Taipa ferry wharf
氹仔輪船碼頭

Causeway-Bridge to Taipa Island

CHINA
中國

Pearl River
珠江

澳門 Macau

Ma Kok Miu
媽閣廟

Rua da Praia do Bairro do Barra

Naval dockyard
政府造船廠

氹仔 Taipa

Barra
Fortress
媽閣炮台

Avenida da República

0 100 200 300 400 m
0 100 200 300 400 500 yards

路環 Coloane

N

of many denominations. But today, if the name of Macau still evokes visions of international intrigue, most of it is to be found only at the gambling tables.

Seeing Macau

Directly across the street from the wharf where passengers arrive from Hong Kong is the first surprise of Macau—the vast new Jai-alai Palace, said to be the world's most luxurious *frontón*. Players of the lightning-fast Basque ball game are imported from Spain to provide something different to bet on.

The grandstand on the seaside road, the Avenida da Amizade (Friendship Avenue), marks the finishing line for the Macau Grand Prix, the international racing car event that takes place every November.

The next landmark is the eye-popping cylindrical Hotel Lisboa, with 600 rooms and a couple of floors of gambling premises (open to the public). The hotel's gaudy architecture has become as much a trademark of the new Macau as the nearby bridge to the island of Taipa, an original and graceful feat of engineering.

Continuing clockwise round the peninsula, the **Rua da Praia Grande** (Big Beach Street) is a pleasant promenade with benches under the banyan trees. Along this elegant avenue is Government House, a modest pink palace.

The 17th-century **Barra fortress,** defending the southern tip of the peninsula, contains the chapel of Santiago (St. James). The saint is much revered locally. Among other legends about the statue is a very modern one. During the Cultural Revolution in China, when Red Guards ran rampant on Wanchai island just a swim away, the image of St. James is said to have stepped down from the altar and halted an invasion. A luxury inn has been built into the fortress.

For a close view of Wanchai—you can almost read the communist wall posters—stroll along the waterfront between the naval dockyard and the Taipa ferry wharf. On the Macau side is the territory's oldest shrine, built before the Portuguese arrived. Ma Kok Miu, or **A Ma Temple,** has developed into a complex of shrines weaving up the Barra hillside. This is the favourite temple of Macau's fishermen.

A very secular shrine, moored on the western waterfront, is the Macau Palace, a floating casino. This fancifully decorated multi-storey barge goes nowhere, and is fitted out with gambling tables, slot machines (known locally as "hungry tigers"), and, for hungry humans, a restaurant.

For an authentic whiff of old Portugal, slip into the cool entrance hall of the **Leal Senado** ("Loyal Senate" building), right on the main street. On the walls are flowered blue tiles *(azulejos)* and noble coats of arms. The inscription over the archway reads, *(Cidade do nome de Deus, não ha outra mais leal)* " City of the Name of God, None is More Loyal"—a bit of praise attributed to Portugal's King John IV in the 17th century. For all its historic grandeur, the loyal Senate now is the equivalent of a city council, its statesmanship dedicated to water supplies, sewage lines and the establishment of playgrounds.

Macau's most memorable monument, the **Ruins of St. Paul's,** is the Baroque façade of a 17th-century Jesuit church. The rest of the building, and an attached college, was destroyed in a typhoon-fanned fire in 1835. The rich sculptural effects on the façade mix eastern and western symbols: familiar saints, Chinese dragons and a Portuguese caravel.

The golden age of Portuguese discoveries was immortalized by Luís Vaz de Camões (1524–80), the national poet, who is believed to have spent some time in Macau. Local legend claims that he wrote part of his great saga, *Os Lusíadas* in what is now called the Camões Grotto of the spacious tropical **Camões Garden.**

Alongside the garden, in an 18th-century mansion, is the local museum, also named in honour of the bard. The **Museu Luís de Camões** has an admirable collection of Chinese ceramics, bronzes and paintings. There are ancient and fascinating statues of people and animals, and 18th-century glazed ceramics with startlingly up-to-date colour schemes. Among the paintings are watercolours of old Macau and oil portraits of Chinese dignitaries.

Next to the museum, behind a gate which is opened to anyone who knocks, is the **Old Protestant Cemetery.** For those who had to die on some far foreign field, a more peaceful, lovely graveyard couldn't have been found. In this carefully tended garden the inscriptions on the tombstones tell exciting, tragic stories, mostly of young men who died in war in the 18th and 19th centuries. The gravestones read like the outline of an adventure novel.

The square which faces the park, the museum and the cemetery serves as the offices of professional scribes, who write letters and fill out documents in Chinese for illiterate clients. They write with plain ballpoint pens; no classical calligraphy at two *patacas* per page.

For a different vision of Old China, spend a few tranquil minutes in the **Lou Lim Ieoc** garden. Arched bridges, pagodas, fish ponds and stands of bamboo create the mood of a timeless Chinese painting. Birds chirp among the jacarandas and weeping willows, and dragonflies swoop over the lotus ponds.

Chinese visitors to Macau are usually taken to the Memorial House of Dr. Sun Yat-sen, founder of the Chinese republic. Photos and documents tell the life story of the physician-revolutionary-statesman, who lived for a time in Macau—but never in this building.

Another "must" for most visitors is **Kun Iam Tong,** a 17th-century Buddhist temple of considerable splendour and charm. Amidst statues, carvings and incense burners, the faithful make their devotions and check their fortunes. Funerary displays give a cheerful send-off to the recently departed. An unexpected histori-

A corner of old Portugal survives alongside the ruins of St. Paul's.

cal angle turns up in the monastery garden, where guides point out a small stone table used for a treaty-signing ceremony in 1844. The signatories were the Chinese viceroy from Canton and the minister plenipotentiary of the United States of America. It was the first treaty ever between the two countries.

The most northerly point in Macau is the frontier between two worlds. The **Barrier Gate** (*Portas do Cerco*), erected more than a century ago, marks the boundary between the capitalist enclave of Macau and the People's Republic of China.

Just north of the border, at GONGBEI, is the starting point for China daytrips and longer excursions to places as distant as Guangzhou (Canton).

Macau's Islands

Bridges now link Macau with both its offshore islands, Taipa and Coloane beyond it. TAIPA is a sparsely inhabited island of duck ponds, fish ponds and fireworks factories. Industrial and resort development goes on at a rapid pace, but life is little changed for the old-time fishermen and farmers.

Pay a visit to the **Taipa Folk Museum** and you'll see how Portuguese families lived in the old days. A grand colonial house with cool verandahs provides the centrepiece for this expanding "cultural village".

Coloane offers the pleasures of sand and sea. CHEOC VAN, a small sandy strand on the south side of the island, boasts a restaurant, swimming pool and changing rooms. HAC SA ("Black Sands") is bigger, with more elaborate facilities.

In the village of Coloane, the waterfront drive parallels the shore of a Chinese island just across the water. You can clearly make out the Chinese houses, watch-towers and pill-boxes. At the far end of the drive is a temple which proudly displays a whalebone sculpture of a boat. Wooden oarsmen have been added, along with a dragon's head for the prow.

A few streets away a monument with cannon balls strewn at the base commemorates a Portuguese victory over pirates in 1910. And a modern Catholic church on the square plays recorded hymns—in Chinese.

Lucky Macau

The non-stop excitement of the casinos involves familiar international games—baccarat, blackjack, boule, craps, roulette—and more exotic Chinese pastimes. Watch the fan-tan dealer for a few minutes and you'll be almost an expert. It's simply a matter of how many odd buttons are left after he has divided a pile of them into groups of four.

Dai-Siu (Big and Small) is a dice game in which the croupier throws three dice inside a glass container. Players bet on the numbers that come up, and whether the result is "big" or "small". *Keno* is a variation of bingo in which the player chooses numbers to bet on before the drawing is made.

There is no admission charge at casinos. Dress is optional: some ladies wear long dresses, some local fishermen wear their working clothes. Employees of the Macau government are barred from the casinos except for three days at the lunar New Year, when some are rumoured to invest their year's savings. A proliferation of pawn shops indicates that not everyone wins.

The casinos keep busy 24 hours a day, but if you have time to spare there are additional gambling opportunities: pari mutuel betting on jai-alai, the high-speed Basque game, greyhound racing at the Canidrome, and harness racing on Taipa island.

Shopping

Browsing is a pleasure in Macau's main streets and by-ways, where shops aimed at tourists are interspersed with iron-mongers, herbalists and noodle stalls. Knowledgeable travellers look for antiques, either Chinese heirlooms or leftovers from the gracious Portuguese colonial days. Jewellery and gold have high priority. Contemporary handicrafts, both Portuguese and Chinese from across the border, are also worth a look.

Food and Drink

Gourmets give Macau high marks for dependable Chinese cooking with an exotic bonus... Portuguese food and wines. Chinese, Portuguese and international-style restaurants serve up hearty meals at economical prices.

The ingredients, especially the fresh fish and seafood, are first-rate. Your chopsticks have never dissected a more delicate, delicious fish than Macau sole (*linguado*). Imported dried cod (*bacalhao*) is the Portuguese national dish; you can try several varieties, usually baked.

Macau has an ample, happily priced supply of Portuguese wines. You can have a *Vinho Verde*, a slightly sparkling young wine from northern Portugal, with your fish, and a hearty red *Dao* or *Colares* with your meat. After dinner: Madeira or Port. For the abstemious, they even sell Portuguese mineral waters.

Macau Memo

Currency: Macau's own currency, the *pataca*, is divided into 100 *avos*. The *pataca* (often abbreviated $ locally) is worth about the same as the Hong Kong dollar, which also circulates widely in Macau. Banks, hotels, money-changing offices and casinos change traveller's cheques and foreign currency. No restrictions on import or export of money.

Customs: Passengers from Macau may return to Hong Kong with one duty-free bottle of wine and 100 cigarettes.

Electric current: Hotels usually provide 220-volt, 50 cycle power, but some areas of Macau are still on 110 volts.

Emergency: Dial 3333 for police, 2222 for fire.

Getting there: Jetfoil, hydrofoil, hoverferry, high-speed ferry and conventional ferry boat services are frequent between Hong Kong and Macau, but advance reservations are advisable at any time—and indispensable for weekends and holidays.

Languages: Cantonese is most people's mother tongue. English is more widely known than Macau's official language, Portuguese, which is mainly used in government bureaus, the courts, etc.

Mini-mokes: These jeep-like vehicles can be hired at the Macau Ferry Terminal. Bring a valid driving licence or an International Driving Permit.

Pedicabs: Used by locals as well as tourists, these bike-propelled taxis have no meters, so it's best to agree on the price in advance.

Post office: Macau postage stamps may by bought at the main post office or in hotels. The red pillar-boxes are marked *Correio*.

Public transport: Several bus routes cover the city as well as the islands. Take the topless yellow double-deck bus to Coloane for sightseeing on the way. Bus stops are marked by a red disc reading *Paragem auto-omnibus.*

Taxis: Metered taxis are abundantly available except at holiday time.

Tourist information offices:

Australia: Macau Tourist Information Bureau, 135 Macquarie Street, Sydney, N.S.W. 2000. Tel.: (02) 241-3334.

Britain: Macau Tourist Information Bureau, Airwork House, 35 Piccadilly, London W1V 9PB. Tel.: (01) 734-7272.

Canada: Macau Tourist Information Bureau, 150 Dundas Street W., Toronto, ON M5G 1Z6. Tel.: (416) 593-1811.

U.S.A.: Macau Tourist Information Bureau, Box 1860, Los Angeles, CA 90078. Tel.: (213) 851-3402. Macau Tourist Information Bureau, 608 Fifth Ave., Suite 309, New York, NY 10020. Tel.: (212) 581-7465.

Hong Kong: Macau Tourist Information Bureau, Shun Tak Centre, 200 Connaught Road Central. Tel.: (5) 40 81 80. There's also an information desk at Hong Kong airport.

In Macau itself, maps and brochures may be obtained from the Department of Tourism and Information, Travessa do Paiva. Tel.: 7 72 18.

Visas: Visitors from most West European countries (including Great Britain) and Australia, Canada, the U.S.A., New Zealand, Japan and the Philippines) are admitted to Macau visa-free. Most others are granted visas automatically on arrival by showing a valid passport and paying the fee. But if your country maintains no diplomatic relations with Portugal, you must apply for a visa in advance from a Portuguese consulate overseas.

When to go: Best climate in spring and autumn. Avoid Chinese New Year and the November Grand Prix, when Macau is jammed.

BERLITZ® GOES VIDEO – *FOR LANGUAGES*

Here's a brand new 90-minute video from Berlitz for learning key words and phrases for your trip. It's easy and fun. Berlitz language video combines computer graphics with live action and freeze frames. You see on your own TV screen the type of dialogue you will encounter abroad. You practice conversation by responding to questions put to you in the privacy of your own living room.

Shot on location for accuracy and realism, Berlitz gently leads you through travel situations towards language proficiency. Available from video stores and selected bookstores and Berlitz Language Centers everywhere. Only $59.95 plus $3.00 for shipping and handling.

To order by credit card, call 1-800-228-2028 Ext. 35.

Coming soon to the U.K.

BERLITZ® GOES VIDEO – *FOR TRAVEL*

Travel Tips from Berlitz – now an invaluable part of the informative and colourful videocassette series of more than 50 popular destinations produced by Travelview International. Ideal for planning a trip or as a souvenir of your visit, Travelview videos provide 40 to 60 minutes of valuable information including a destination briefing, a Reference Guide to local hotels and tourist attractions plus practical Travel Tips from Berlitz.

Available from leading travel agencies and video stores everywhere in the U.S.A. and Canada or call 1-800-325-3108 (Texas, call (713) 975-7077; 1-800 661 9269 in Canada). Coming soon to the U.K.

Travelview
INTERNATIONAL
5630 Beverly Hill
Houston, Texas 77057

Border Zones

For Hong Kong visitors with little time to spare for planning or sightseeing, various tour agencies run daytrips to the area just across the border for a hint of the "real" China. Although the farm country is typically Chinese, the city of Shenzhen is not; as part of a special economic zone devised to attract foreign investment, its standard of living is far higher than average. Daytrips across the frontier from Macau typically visit the village of Cuiheng, birthplace of Dr. Sun Yat-sen.

Guangzhou (Canton)

Although it's the most-visited city in China, Guangzhou (or Canton, as it is much better known abroad) can hardly be considered blasé about tourists. Overseas visitors are still objects of intense curiosity, even if they no longer draw a crowd.

Foreigners have been turning up in Guangzhou for a couple of thousand years, for it was the country's first major seaport. This has made for some dramatic historical incidents: the Opium Wars, for instance, broke out because of a

GUANGZHOU
(CANTON) 广州

crackdown in Canton. But the city maintains its gateway role. Ever since 1957 the Canton Trade Fair (officially the Chinese Export Commodities Fair) has attracted throngs of international business people every spring and autumn. Even when tourism dwindled almost to zero because of political upheavals, Guangzhou kept open the nation's ties with foreign countries and with overseas Chinese.

Guangzhou (population around five million) straddles the Pearl River, China's fifth longest river, which links the city to the South China Sea. The waterway accounts for much of the local charm and excitement: the daily drama of ferryboats, junks, sampans, freighters—even small tankers and big gunboats—right in the centre of town. The river also irrigates surrounding farmlands, so lush and carefully tended that the subtropical scene gladdens the heart.

What to See

Package tours to Guangzhou—the easy way to China—have a fairly standard itinerary. But there is no objection if you want to leave a specific excursion and roam on your own within the city limits. A typical four-day schedule contains sightseeing by coach and boat, excursions to a farming community or an industrial town, a theatre outing and a full-scale Chinese banquet.

You can also travel independently by bus from Hong Kong.

When it comes to sightseeing sensations, Guangzhou doesn't claim to be in the same league as Beijing or Xi'an. But its monuments and parks are well worth visiting, not least for the chance to mingle with the Cantonese themselves.

Yuexiu Park, near the Trade Fair in the northern part of the city, covers a hilly 229 acres. Along with pretty gardens, lakes and sports facilities, Guangzhou's largest park contains one of the city's oldest buildings, **Zhenhai Tower.** Actually, "tower" is a misleading description for a verandahed building of five storeys, but owing to its hilltop position it did serve as an ancient watchtower. Built in 1380, it now houses the municipal museum, with em- **67**

phasis on Guangzhou's history and art.

An equally famous but modern landmark in the park is a granite sculptural representation of five handsome goats. Legend says five gods descended from heaven riding upon goats which held sprigs of rice in their mouths. The celestial visitors distributed the rice, blessing the local people with eternal freedom from famine. The gods thereupon disappeared, according to the story, but the five rice-bearing goats turned to stone.

Dr. Sun Yat-sen (1866–1925), who began his political career in Canton, is honoured in Yuexiu Park by an **obelisk** about 100 feet tall. South of the park is an even more impressive **monument** to him, built in 1931 with contributions from overseas Chinese.

Tourists of all ages convene at Guangzhou's Zhenhai Tower.

This vast, modern version of a traditional Chinese building, with its sweeping blue tile roofs, contains an auditorium big enough to seat close to 5,000 people.

Guangzhou's prime Buddhist monument, the **Temple of the Six Banyan Trees,** was founded more than 1,400 years ago. The trees which inspired an 11th-century poet and calligrapher to rename the Precious Solemnity Temple have died, but the often-restored complex remains a focus of local Buddhist activities. Overlooking it all is the 17-storey **Flower Pagoda,** a slender relic of the Song dynasty (A.D. 960-1279).

In the early Middle Ages, Canton had a significant Muslim population thanks to trade with the Middle East. This explains the presence in Guangzhou of the **Huaisheng Mosque,** said to be China's oldest mosque, traditionally dated A.D. 627. It has been rebuilt in modern times and, after a hiatus during the Cultural Revolution, again serves the small local community of Muslims. The modern **minaret** is known colloquially as the Plain (or Naked) Pagoda, in contrast to the Ornate Pagoda of the nearby Buddhist temple.

Another religious edifice that went through hard times in the 1960s and 70s is the Roman Catholic **Cathedral.** Red Guards converted the century-old Gothic church into a warehouse, but the cathedral was reconsecrated in 1979.

The feeling of 19th-century Canton is best evoked by **Shamian island,** in the Pearl River, linked to central Guangzhou by two bridges. This small residential island, beautifully shaded by banyan trees, was the closed community of the foreign colony in the era of the "concessions". The stately European-style buildings have been taken over as government offices, foreign legations or public housing. The churches have been assigned the most prosaic uses; one is a warehouse with pews. Note the stained-glass windows acquired by nearby houses. The island, haunted with nostalgia, has a fresh claim to touristic attention: a big modern luxury hotel.

A popular, optional excursion is an hour's detour to the **Guangzhou Zoo,** founded in 1958. More than 200 animal species are represented, most famously the giant panda. The zoo also has an imaginative monkey mountain behind a moat.

Revolutionary Monuments

Guided tours of Guangzhou usually include one or more of the sites linked with revolutionary activity in the city's history:

The **National Peasant Movement Institute,** housed in a former Confucian temple, was where the Chinese Communist Party trained its corps of leaders in the 1920s. Mao Zedong himself directed the institute in 1926; another teacher here was Zhou Enlai.

Martyrs Memorial Park—more formally the Memorial Park to the Martyrs of the Guangzhou Uprising—was dedicated on the 30th anniversary of the doomed insurrection of December 11, 1927. The armed uprising against the Kuomintang, led by the Communist Party, was crushed within three days at a cost of more than 5,000 lives. Most of the park consists of lawns and flower gardens, palm trees and pavilions, so it's an unexpectedly relaxed place to watch the locals strolling, courting, or playing Chinese checkers.

Another memorial park surrounds the **Mausoleum of the 72 Martyrs,** dedicated to victims of one of the insurrections that failed in 1911, only months before Dr. Sun Yat-sen's successful revolution.

Excursion

The most popular daytrip from Guangzhou goes to **Foshan,** a city of nearly 300,000, renowned over the centuries for its handicrafts. Among the tourist stops here are a factory where silk is woven, a ceramics plant, and the Foshan Folk Art

Studio, where workers may be watched making Chinese lanterns, carving sculptures, painting scrolls and cutting intricate designs in paper. (Shopping opportunities are always provided.)

Foshan's most outstanding artistic monument is the Taoist **Ancestral Temple,** a

Revolution failed to dim age-old Chinese emphasis on good food.

Song dynasty establishment rebuilt in the 14th century. It is a work of extravagant beauty, uniting many ancient art forms, in wood, brick, stone, ceramics and bronze.

Guangzhou Memo

Banks and currency exchange: Foreign currency and traveller's cheques may be exchanged in hotels and Friendship Stores. Take your passport along. Keep the receipt in case you want to change excess money back to foreign currency when leaving the country.

Currency: Chinese "people's money", called *renminbi* (RMB), is based on the *yuan,* divided into 100 *fen.* Ten fen make a *jiao.* However, a two-tier currency scheme allots foreigners a separate kind of money called Foreign Exchange Certificates (FEC), issued in denominations of 1 and 5 jiao (= 10 and 50 fen) and 1, 5, 10, 50 and 100 yuan. Friendship Stores, hotels and other establishments catering to foreigners accept only FEC, not RMB.

Customs: China sets liberal quotas on the amount of cigarettes, wine and film you can bring with you, but restrictions affect reading

matter, radio transmitters, weapons, etc. Ask for the latest regulations when you apply for your visa.

Driving: Unlike Hong Kong, China drives on the right. Drive-yourself cars are not available for hire.

Electric current: 220-volt, 50-cycle A.C.

Getting there: Several daily flights link Hong Kong and Guangzhou. Train travellers can cover the distance in less than three hours aboard de luxe expresses. Cheaper, conventional trains require a stopover at the border, where passengers walk across to meet another train. Another way of travelling is the regular hovercraft service from Tai Kok Tsui (Kowloon) to the port of Whampoa.

Language: Though Cantonese is the local dialect (as in Hong Kong), a substantial proportion of the people speak the national language, *putonghua* (known abroad as Mandarin). Hotel staff know some English.

Photography: Prohibited at the border. It is forbidden to film military objects, soldiers, industrial establishments, etc.

Public transport: Buses and trolley-buses cover the major routes. Tourists are more likely to use taxis, which are best ordered through the hotel.

Restaurants: Note that dinner hours are earlier than in many countries—6 to 7.30 p.m. on average.

Shopping hours: Usually from 9 a.m. to 7 p.m., seven days a week.

Tipping: Not permitted. But a small gift to, say, a tour guide would not be out of place.

Tourist information offices: For information on travel to China, consult a Chinese embassy or consulate or one of the following:
Great Britain: China Tourist Office, 4 Glentworth St., London N.W.1.
U.S.A.: China International Travel Service, 60 E. 42nd St., New York, N.Y. 10165.
Hong Kong: China International Travel Service, South Sea Centre, 75 Mody Rd., Tsim Sha Tsui East. Tel.: (3) 7215317, or
China Travel Service (H.K.) Ltd., 77 Queens Road, Central. Tel.: (5) 259121.

Visa: Certain approved travel agents as well as China International Travel Service expedite matters in as little as 24 hours.

Water: Avoid tap water everywhere in China. But you can safely drink the boiled (for tea-making) water in hotel-room thermos flasks.

What to Do

Shopping

Though inflation takes its toll here as elsewhere, Hong Kong's reputation for bargains is well-founded. But the biggest difference between Hong Kong and other duty-free ports is the stupendous choice.

The favourite buys in Hong Kong fall into two categories: duty-free imported goods, on which you benefit by saving your own country's luxury tax, and merchandise, usually hand-made, from Hong Kong and China. In the first class are cameras and lenses, hi-fi equipment and watches. The "software" includes Oriental souvenirs and men's suits and shirts run up by those deft Hong Kong tailors.

When and Where

Major shops in Hong Kong are open from 9 or 10 a.m. to 6 or 7 p.m. daily except Sunday. But in Kowloon and Causeway Bay, for instance, shopping continues until 9.30 or 10 p.m., Sunday included.

The only holiday on which all commerce comes to a halt is the Chinese New Year in January or February.

Prices are about the same in Hong Kong and Kowloon. Big shops on fashionable thoroughfares tend to be more expensive than "family" shops tucked away in side streets.

For unusual shopping, don't miss the street markets with their unexpected bargains. For a cross-section of handicrafts, visit the shopping centres pat-

terned after traditional Chinese villages. Artisans on duty demonstrate wood carving, calligraphy and other talents. The Communist Chinese department stores, which have "sales" and smiles just like capitalist shops, sell fascinating merchandise at attractive prices. Look for art, toys and food.

Buyer Beware

The large department stores post their prices, which are fixed. But elsewhere you should ask whether there is a discount. In many shops haggling is the

Buyers tiptoe through temptations in Hollywood Road antique shop.

order of the day, but it's pointless if you're ill-informed. Never buy any significant item without a thorough comparison-shopping investigation; it's a good idea to know what it costs at home, too. Beware of improbable bargains: if the price goes absurdly low you may be buying stolen or falsely labelled goods. Ask for the manufacturer's guarantee on watches, hi-fi and photo equipment.

In haggling, the merchant assumes you are prepared to pay cash. If, after concluding a deal, you try to pay with a credit card, he may boost the price to cover the card charges. Beware of touts who promise to take you to wondrous bargains. And ignore any shopkeeper who accosts you from his doorway. Note that alcohol, tobacco and perfume are exceptions to Hong Kong's duty-free régime and are subject to tax.

What to Buy

Antiques. The Hollywood Road area is a centre of antique dealers, but there are others in all the tourist shopping zones. Fine Chinese bronzes, embroidery, lacquerware, porcelain and wood carving, among other possibilities, may be found. Experts point out that the age of a Chinese antique is not the only factor to consider, as dynasties had their creative ups and downs. Haggling as such is frowned upon but discounts can often be obtained. Meanwhile, beware of convincing modern imitations masquerading as real antiques.

Brocades and silks. Fabrics from China, inexpensive raw silk or exquisite brocades, are well worth taking home for later use. The Chinese department stores also sell silk scarves, ties, and ready-made blouses with fine embroidery work.

Calculators. Miniaturization multiplies the convenience of these electronic marvels, while Hong Kong subtracts tax from the price. It's hard to resist joining the post-abacus bandwagon.

Cameras. Photo buffs all know that Hong Kong is the place for bargains, and it's true. But be sure to compare prices and models before you buy.

Carpets and rugs. Hong Kong is a mecca for Chinese handknotted wool carpets and silk rugs, and most stores arrange for shipping.

China. In Hong Kong you can have a plate—or a whole dinner service—handpainted to your own design. Factories in Kowloon and the New Territories, producing traditional and modern china, are geared to

entertain and instruct visiting tourists; prices are appealing. In antique shops, look for highly valued porcelains from China. Surprisingly, good bargains may be found among the best European china—Spode, Wedgwood and the like—because of the duty-free situation.

Diamonds. Thanks to the duty-free clause, and low overheads, diamonds sell at favourable prices on the Hong Kong market, one of the world's biggest diamond exchanges. Most laymen are incapable of judging nuances of colour, purity and workmanship which can seriously affect a gem's resale value; all the more reason not

Sculpture due for sale in Hong Kong receives final touches in workshop across border in China.

to do your diamond-buying in a back alley, but to seek out a reputable dealer.

Gold. The Chinese are keen on gold, both as jewellery and as an investment. Bullion dealers sell it by the *tael* (1.33 ounces) at a price which varies according to the world's woes. You can buy it by the bar or in finished ornamental form; choose the shop carefully.

Hi-fi, stereo, etc. Audio fans revel in the vast variety of rigs on show at interesting prices. **77**

With all the world's speakers, tape decks, turntables and gimmicks on sale, be sure to have a good look around before you hand over your fortune. As with cameras, dealers naturally try to sell last year's models before this year's. In either case, it's often possible to work out a discount.

Ivory. Beautiful reproductions of intricate Chinese carvings are sold in many shops. But proceed with caution, for only an expert can tell the difference between a genuine tusk and substitute material.

Jade. "Good for the health" is just one among other magical qualities attributed to these emerald green or turquoise stones. This explains the constant demand which keeps prices up. You may be offered counterfeit jade, which looks

Ignoring Hong Kong bargains in electronic calculators, merchant does his sums on Chinese abacus.

exactly like the genuine article. Some say you can test the authenticity by touch: real jade feels smooth and cool. Or you can shine a lamp on the stone: real jade shows no reflected light. Or you can lick it: real jade makes the tongue feel numb. Better still, go shopping with an expert, or patronize a respectable shop.

Lighters. In the absence of any luxury tax, gold cigarette lighters and other fancy smokers' accessories fall into the bargain category in Hong Kong. Look over the range of expensive imported pipes, too.

Luggage. The practical way to get all those gifts home is to buy an extra suitcase on the spot. There are plenty to choose from in all sizes and styles, including famous name brands at reasonable prices. Best buys: Hong Kong imitations of luxury models, and Chinese-made suitcases—unfashionable but sturdy and cheap.

Mah-jong sets. Ivory sets are extremely expensive but even tiles of bone or plastic have a certain charm when they've been engraved by hand. As you'll know from the clickety-clack behind every second window in Hong Kong, mah-jong is one of the most popular local vices.

Musical instruments. The Chinese department stores sell extremely cheap guitars as well as those exotic stringed instruments which carry the tune at Chinese opera performances.

Oriental oddments. There's no end to the curiosities you'll come across as you make the rounds of antique shops, specialist boutiques and back street pushcarts: an old Chinese coin, an abacus, a bird cage, a tiny set of scales, a cricket cage, a kite, a collapsible fan, an old snuff bottle … and so on.

Paintings. Chinese artists still devote themselves to copying classic paintings. Calligraphic scrolls are also highly regarded. Competing for the tourist dollar are art factories mass-producing oil paintings of Hong Kong scenes, or of any other subject that will sell.

Pearls. A very good buy in Hong Kong, especially those without the burden of brand names. But if you don't have the expertise, better put your trust in a reputable shop.

Perfumes. A big selection in Hong Kong at favourable prices. To avoid counterfeits or stale scents, patronize the major shops.

Ready-to-wear clothes. Hong Kong is one of the world's top producers—for export. Not much is left over for local sale, but it's worth looking for. Fac-

cheap, but the fabrics and workmanship combine to make a good investment. Eminently worthwhile for hard-to-fit customers who hate baggy off-the-rack shirts.

Tailoring. Nimble gnomes no longer sit up all night producing those 24-hour suits for transit passengers, but local tailors can still be hurried, up to a point. As a rule, the more time you allow them, the better the product. At the least, expect to undergo two or three fittings over three or four days. The result can be a suit of admirable quality at a fair price—though made-to-measure clothing is no longer cheap these days.

Tea. Shops all over town, doling out tea leaves to enthusiastic local customers, will sell you gift tins of exotic blends.

Toys. Almost all of Hong Kong's toys are exported. But cheap and fascinating toys can still be found everywhere including the Communist Chinese department stores.

Umbrellas. Any time there's a shower, umbrella hawkers appear on almost every corner. Local products are cheap and effective, in collapsible or conventional designs.

Watches. Time is money in Hong Kong: shoppers spend more on watches and clocks

tory rejects or over-production may wind up on pushcarts in "native" markets at delightfully slashed prices.

Shoes. With typical deftness, bootmakers are ready to custom-make any model you fancy.

Shirts. Men's hand-made
shirts are no longer exactly

than on cameras and optical goods. Most duty-free havens have watch bargains, but in Hong Kong the advantage is the enormous variety of makes and models: Swiss, Japanese, American, luxury or utilitarian styles are all on sale. Don't buy from a tout on a street-corner and be sure you get the manufacturer's guarantee, properly signed and sealed.

Wine. The Chinese department stores sell a staggering variety of wines and spirits, from snake wine to knockout potions. They come in anything ranging from hair-tonic bottles to charming gift flasks.

Woks (circular pans), and any other gadgets essential to Chinese cookery—now that you're a fan. Department stores sell all sorts of intriguing kitchen aids.

Outdoor jade market, opposite, and food store typify endless variety of shopping thrills in Hong Kong.

Sports

Water Sports

In subtropical Hong Kong you can swim from April to early November. Forty "official" beaches—manned by lifeguards and equipped with at least basic facilities—are found on the south and east coasts of Hong Kong island, in the New Territories and on three offshore islands. In addition there are countless isolated beaches reachable only by boat. On summer weekends the "official" beaches become uncomfortably overpopulated. (Repulse Bay has been known to pack in 45,000 bodies on a summer Sunday.) But the crowds are much less oppressive on weekdays and at the beginning and end of the season.

If Repulse Bay or the New Territories are too far to go for a swim, consider the public pools in Victoria Park or Kowloon Tsai Park.

Underwater swimming. Hong Kong's coral and tropical fish are best seen far from the

Exercise in fast and slow motion: Finish line at Sha Tin, tai-chi enthusiasts in Victoria Park.

82

centres of population. For information and advance planning on how to get to the best diving areas, write to Hong Kong Underwater Federation, GPO Box 9012, Hong Kong, or YMCA Scuba Club, c/o YMCA, Salisbury Road, Kowloon, Hong Kong. For last minute arrangements try the Sea Dragon Skin Diving Club, Tel. (5) 72 16 29.

Sailing. Owing to the intensive traffic in the harbour, only sailors licensed by the Hong Kong authorities are permitted to run pleasure boats in local waters. But it's possible to hire a crewed junk. Check with the Tourist Association for details.

Water-skiing. Best bet is to reserve a boat, with operator and skis included, from the Deep Water Bay Speed Boat Co., Tel. (5) 92 03 91. They're at the beach just north-west of Repulse Bay.

Sports Ashore
Golf. Some of the big hotels can arrange guest privileges at courses of the Royal Hong Kong Golf Club, but only Mondays to Fridays. The biggest concentration of golf courses, at Fanling in the New Territories, is about an hour's train ride from the Kowloon terminal.

84 **Ice-skating.** A change of mood after a torrid summer day: the big indoor rink at Lai Chi Kok Amusement Park or at City Plaza, Taikoo Shing, Quarry Bay.

Riding. On Lantau island (near Po Lin Monastery) and in the New Territories at the Sha Tin Riding School, Tel. (0) 61 39 10.

Tennis. First come, first served at the public courts at Victoria Park, Kowloon Tsai Park and Bowen Road, except for Saturdays and Sundays which can be booked a week in advance.

Spectator Sports
Horse racing. High society and everybody else share a feverish interest in the Sport of Kings. Hong Kong maintains two tracks—the traditional Happy Valley course on Hong Kong island and the striking new Sha Tin establishment in the New Territories.

Cricket. The action has moved from the old pitch, incongruously located in the shadow of the Communist Chinese bank to new quarters in Wong-Nei-Chong Gap Road. Across the harbour, the Kowloon Cricket Club plays at a ground in Cox's Road.

Football. From late September to early May, football (soccer) is the most popular sport.

Museums

Hong Kong Museum of Art, City Hall, 10th and 11th floors. Rotating exhibitions provide a crash course in Chinese ceramics, bronzes, jade, paintings —including pictures documenting Sino-British relations.

Hong Kong Space Museum, Salisbury Road, Kowloon, contains a planetarium and exhibition hall, offering shows on timely interplanetary themes.

Fung Ping Shan Museum of Hong Kong University, 94 Bonham Road, Hong Kong. From ancient Chinese pottery to nearly a thousand early Christian crosses, plus paintings, sculpture and bronzes.

Hong Kong Museum of History, Kowloon Park. A brief survey of local culture and customs from prehistory to modern times, illustrating everything from fishing techniques and farming to architecture and handicrafts.

Museum of Chinese Historical Relics, 1st floor, Causeway Centre, 28 Harbour Road, Wanchai. Displays of cultural treasures from China, with temporary exhibitions from specific provinces twice a year.

Flagstaff House Museum of Tea Ware, Victoria Barracks, Cotton Tree Drive, Hong Kong, houses an unusual collection of Chinese tea sets dating from the 5th century B.C. to the present.

Lei Cheng Uk Museum, Tonkin Street, Kowloon. Ancient history discovered inside a hillock during construction of a crowded complex of seven-storey tenements: a 2,000-year-old Han tomb, now protected behind glass. In the small museum you can view funerary objects found on the site.

For museum opening hours, see p. 116.

Festivals

Religious or secular, joyful or pompous, festivals give every year its landmarks and momentum. Hong Kong's calendar is full of holidays which mirror British and Chinese traditions. Some highlights of colourful culture:

Lunar New Year (January or February). Now mostly a family celebration. Everything in Hong Kong, even business, shuts down for the duration. A time for paying debts, dressing up, and giving gifts. With fireworks banned, the most all-pervasive motif for the holiday is the flowers. Peach blossoms, narcissus and miniature orange trees overwhelm the markets).

Ching Ming Festival (April).

This family holiday is timed to the solar calendar (unlike most Chinese festivals—and Easter —which are pegged to the lunar calendar). Known as the Festival for Sweeping of Graves, Ching Ming's ancestor worship is not all as solemn as it sounds.

Birthday of Tin Hau (April or May). The Taoist Goddess of the Sea is honoured by Hong Kong's fisherfolk with prayers for safe voyages and good catches. Liveliest celebration is at isolated Joss House Bay, where brightly decorated junks and sampans converge with offerings. Spectators can reach the beach by special excursion boats. Smaller-scale celebrations, including lion-dancing, take place at other Tin Hau temples in the colony, notably at Aberdeen.

Cheung Chau Bun Festival

Making a splash in the traditional way at the Dragon Boat Festival.

(May). The small, unspoiled offshore island of Cheung Chau celebrates its own thanksgiving holiday with roots going back to pirate days. Brilliant, costumed parades in an all-out carnival atmosphere. At midnight on the final day of festivities, hundreds of islanders scramble for good-luck buns. (The exact date of this holiday is impossible to compute in advance, for it is decided by the village elders a few weeks before the event.)

Dragon Boat Festival (May or June). This gala occasion, on the fifth day of the fifth moon, is said to commemorate the tragic watery death of an ancient Chinese statesman-poet, Chu Yuan. Crowds of oarsmen in long, thin dragon boats race splashily to the beat of big bass drums and Chinese gongs. Winning local crews later compete against international dragon-boat teams.

Mid-Autumn Festival (September or October). This one is a children's favourite. As the full moon rises over Hong Kong, tots carrying paper lanterns of traditional or space-age design congregate in open or high places to admire the poetic sight. They eat "moon cakes" (ground sesame and lotus seeds or dates, perhaps enriched with duck egg) and take full advantage of being allowed to stay up late.

Cheung Yeung Festival (October). Nineteen centuries ago, it is said, a man headed for the hills on the advice of a fortune-teller. When he returned he found he was the sole survivor of a calamity. On the ninth day of the ninth moon (the day of the disaster), Hong Kong people visit the hillside graves of their ancestors and try to reach some "high place" for luck.

87

Folklore

Chinese opera. To the foreigner, this art form is likely to remain inscrutable even after a couple of exposures. But everyone appreciates the glittering costumes and the clear difference between heroes and villains. The music, though strange to the unaccustomed ear, won't put you to sleep; cymbals and drums guarantee your alertness.

Cantonese opera or the more traditional Peking version is presented frequently at Hong Kong festivals, in theatres and public parks, and nightly at Lai Chi Kok amusement park.

Lion dances. Agile young men in symbolic lion costumes romp to the tune of gongs and drums. It happens at almost any festival or even to enliven the proceedings at official ceremonies.

Dragon dances involve squads of performers inhabiting the flexible "body" of a long, fierce dragon. If a dignitary is in attendance, he or she is invited to "dot the eyes" of the dragon's face with a brush, giving symbolic life to the festive monster.

Puppet shows. Suspended on strings, elevated on rods, worn as gloves or cast as shadows on screens, Chinese puppets and marionettes reproduce all the conventions of the old-fashioned operas. Shows of one or another type, delighting children and adults alike, are often offered free at public parks and playgrounds.

Arts and Culture

Hong Kong Arts Festival. Every February the territory absorbs a dose of culture: concerts, recitals, plays, jazz, Chinese opera and other productions by leading talents from East and West. Tickets must be reserved well in advance.

Festival of Asian Arts. For a fortnight in October Hong Kong plays host to orchestras, dance troupes, opera companies and drama ensembles from all over the Far East. For those who can't get tickets, many supplementary, free performances are staged in the open air.

Music, theatre, dance. Much of the year the City Hall cultural complex and the Arts Centre and Hong Kong Academy for the Performing Arts in Wanchai keep up a steady output of recitals, concerts and plays by local and over-

In Chinese opera, costumes and grimaces help the uninitiated to follow subtle twists in the plot.

seas artists. The Hong Kong Philharmonic Orchestra, a professional organization with an international membership, performs regularly.

Nightlife

Hong Kong by night can match any taste—riotous, sedate, raw or cultured. You may find ro-

mance afloat under a sub-tropical moon—or in a dark, smoky fleshpot. You can dress up for a nightclub or down to watch a street-corner opera. A night out in Hong Kong is as glamorous or earthy as your mood.

Tours. Excursion firms operate several different nightlife tours sampling the more elegant entertainment possibilities. These give the newcomer a head-start in the study of Hong Kong nightlife. They're handy and quite respectable for any tourists, such as unaccompanied women, who might otherwise feel ill at ease on the nightclub circuit. Since the package is paid for in advance, no one need worry about unexpected budgetary bombshells. Some tours combine a Chinese banquet and a gala show, perhaps adding a visit to an open-air market and the panorama from Victoria Peak. In another variation, dinner and dancing is offered aboard an air-conditioned floating nightclub.

Nightclubs. Hong Kong's most distinguished nightclubs, in the principal hotels, have bands, dancing and floor shows, sometimes featuring international stars. Some hotels, and many a nearby basement, also have discothèques where

the lights keep flashing until 2 or 3 a.m.

Bars. For the atmosphere of a Hong Kong honky-tonk, follow the neon glare to Wanchai or Tsim Sha Tsui. Visiting sailors report that the hostess-and-topless scene here is a bit mild compared with some other Asian ports. Be sure to pay for each round of drinks as they are served, lest painful surprises have a chance to multiply.

Other bars. For a quiet drink or snack with perhaps a bit of music, in a non-girlie-bar atmosphere, many British- or Australian-style pubs are available.

Hostess Clubs. The Japanese tourist influx has inspired a growth of nightspots in which hostesses chat with the clients at a standard hourly rate. What with the cover charge and the price of drinks, a radiogram would cost you less per word of conversation.

Poor Man's Nightclub. In a car park near the Macau ferry, a night out with a constant floor show can cost less than the price of a drink in a hotel bar. With the cars all gone after 8 p.m., you can join the crowd for dinner *al fresco* at a noodle stall, be entertained by singers and dancers who pass the hat for contributions, and have your fortune told by a palmist or a little bird. Among the outdoor shopping bargains: tape cassettes and T-shirts. You can even have a suit made. Another animated night market operates in Temple Street, near Jordan Road, Kowloon.

Cinemas. Seats may be booked in advance for separate showings, usually at 2.30, 5.30, 7.30 and 9.30 p.m. English-language films have Chinese subtitles; when locally produced films have Mandarin dialogue they require both English and Chinese subtitles (for the benefit of the large Cantonese-speaking Hong Kong audiences).

Latest fad in Suzie Wong's old town is an outbreak of toplessness.

Wining and Dining

The Chinese invented *haute cuisine.* They still care about food with a passion only the French begin to rival.

In Hong Kong the chefs, following distinguished traditions, aim to please a most demanding clientele. They use the best ingredients, fresh from local farms and the sea. You would have to search high and low to find a bad Chinese meal in this gourmet's wonderland.

The big problem in Hong Kong is how to choose among the thousands of restaurants. Menus are not normally posted outside, so a certain amount of guesswork is involved. But you can get an idea from a restaurant's windows, which may display live fish in tanks, snakes or frogs in cages, or dressed poultry hanging from hooks. Of course, elegant decor and head-waiters, hat-check girls and supernumeraries mean the same as anywhere else in the world: fancier prices.

Even in the Chinese equivalent of a local café there may be hundreds of items on the menu. Let the waiter help you to choose just the right amount of food with the best range of tastes and textures. The more people in your party the better, since everyone shares all the dishes, increasing the opportunities for discovery.

Chinese food comes in half a dozen principal styles, as different from one another as German cooking is from Mexican. In Hong Kong you'll also find a large number of restaurants offering other Asian cuisines. And when you long

for a familiar menu, you'll find plenty of western-style restaurants capable of dishing up a steak, a pizza, or fish and chips.

Meal Times
Hotels serve American, British or continental breakfast from about 7 to 10 a.m. At lunch time businessmen throng the restaurants from 1 to 3 p.m., and families go to dinner between 7.30 and 9.30 p.m. But Chinese restaurants maintain much more flexible timetables;

Eating on the job or on the town, Chinese pursue culinary excellence.

many are open from breakfast time till midnight or later without a break.

While you're waiting for your scrambled eggs, the Chinese are devouring their traditional breakfast: *congee*, a highly digestible rice gruel or porridge to which almost anything may be added, from fried batter to salted fish. At back-street breakfast stalls you'll also see early risers digging into noodle soup with hunks of vegetable or pork.

Dim Sum

Late breakfast or lunch can consist of tea and *dim sum*, the small snacks which add up to a delicious, filling meal. Servers wander from table to table chanting the Cantonese names of the foods contained in their trays or carts. Choose whatever looks interesting as it's offered—spring rolls, spare ribs, dumplings and so on. The comings and goings of clients, tea-waiters and *dim sum* distributors creates the atmosphere of a bazaar, so prepare for an exciting rather than a relaxing lunch. When you ask for the bill the waiter computes it on the basis of the number of empty dishes on the table. Unless you accidentally ordered a rare delicacy, you'll be happily surprised at the low total price.

Floating Food

Another novel eating experience is lunch or dinner afloat. Aboard the big floating restaurants of Aberdeen, fresh seafood is enhanced by the general nautical atmosphere. An even more adventurous way to dine at sea begins any fine evening at the Causeway Bay Typhoon Shelter. You can hire a sampan (a bit dear) and be rowed out to a fleet of floating kitchens which offer to cook their specialities on the spot. The sampans are comfortably equipped with table and chairs. When you're thirsty the drinks sampan will pull alongside; to add romance, engage the floating troubadours for a round of songs.

Food and the Chinese

For the Chinese, eating is a pleasure full of philosophical profundities. Even the dead are offered food and wine for a more peaceful journey from this life.

Perhaps food is so greatly valued because of memories of hard times in the historical or recent past. The common Cantonese greeting is *"Nei sik jo fan mai a?"*—"Have you had your rice yet?" In eras of hunger the Chinese learned to make the most of foods that others might

Chopsticks: Have a Go

You'll lose face—and fun—if you don't learn to use chopsticks in Hong Kong.

First settle the bottom stick firmly at the conjunction of thumb and forefinger, balancing it against the first joint of the ring finger. The second stick pivots around the fulcrum made by the tip of the thumb and the inside of the forefinger. If the sticks were parallel they would be wide enough to pick up an ice-cube; more often they meet at an acute angle.

If it's any consolation, many Chinese don't feel quite at home with knife and fork.

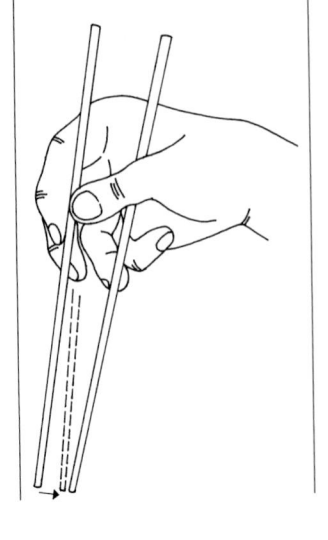

have deemed inedible—serpents, bizarre fish and even the lining gathered from swallows' nests.

Chinese gourmets demand the best flavours plus the subtle factors which enhance the pleasure of food—colour, texture and presentation. And so a proper Chinese meal is orchestrated. There must be a harmonious progression from the sweet to the sour, the crunchy to the tender, the yellow of the pineapple to the red of the pepper. A Chinese banquet is a triumph of the well-rounded art of food.

Regional Cuisines

In a country as big as China regional styles of cooking were bound to develop. Some ingredients were readily available in one area and not another; tastes differed from place to place. In Hong Kong restaurants every major school of Chinese cooking is represented, as Hong Kong has inherited recipes and brilliant cooks from all parts of China. Since most of the residents of the colony have roots just across the border in the area of Guangzhou, the majority of restaurants are Cantonese. (They are not labelled Cantonese any more than a French restaurant in Paris would advertise its **95** nationality.) Cantonese also comes first in alphabetical order, which is how we'll proceed.

Cantonese. For most visitors, this is the most familiar of Chinese cuisines. The Cantonese emigrated to far-off shores, opened restaurants and introduced new tastes to the daring diners of the West; but be ready for new sensations in Hong Kong, where the cooks have all the authentic ingredients.

Steaming or quick stir-frying captures the natural flavour—as well as the colour and vitamins—in Cantonese food. The range of ingredients is vast, the flavours are many and often delicately understated.

Garoupa with ginger and spring onion (羌葱蒸石斑): a popular, meaty, local fish steamed in the company of ginger, spring onions and soya sauce with a touch of garlic.

Sweet and sour prawns (吉列蝦球): shelled fresh prawns in the classic sauce of sugar, vinegar, soya and ketchup, coloured with crisp red and green peppers and pineapple chunks.

Lemon chicken (檸檬軟雞): fried chunks of tender chicken in a creamy sauce of sugared lemon juice and chicken broth.

Crabmeat and corn soup (蟹蓉粟米羹): morsels of crab and kernels of maize in a thick, hearty soup. The Chinese usually have soup towards the end of the meal, but no one will be shocked if you want to begin with it. One exception is shark's fin soup (紅燒鮑翅), which comes in the middle of a meal because it is so special. This thick soup, which the Chinese adore for its texture as much as its taste, may contain mushrooms, chicken, and bacon or ham as well as shark's fin.

Steamed white rice is normally served with a Cantonese meal, although you can order fried rice instead.

Chiu Chow. This cuisine from the Swatow region of south-east China excels in novel seasonings and rich sauces.

Minced pigeon (鴿鬆): the pigeon meat is minced and fried with herbs; you eat it wrapped in lettuce leaves. In Chiu Chow restaurants *congee* (rice porridge) is often served instead of steamed rice. Before and after dinner you will be presented with tiny cups of a strong, bitter tea known as Iron Buddha.

Lunch in a first-class Hong Kong restaurant begins with steamed dumplings in their bamboo trays.

Hakka. The name Hakka means "guest people", referring to their migration to this part of the world from northern China many centuries ago. Hakka cuisine makes the most of simple ingredients, notably the versatile bean curd. Look for an ingenious dish called salted chicken (鹽焗雞); a coating of salt contains and increases the flavours while the bird is being baked.

Peking. Chinese emperors made Peking the gourmet centre of their country, and Hong Kong's Peking restaurants still manage many "Imperial" banquets (ordered in advance) with everything from nuts to soup, in that order. Along the way you won't want to miss one of the world's great eating experiences, Peking Duck (北京填鴨). The duck, honey-coated before roasting, is cut at the table. The celebrants put chunks of the crisp skin and tender flesh, along with spring onions and a sweet sauce, on to delicate pancakes, which are then rolled up and devoured.

Another Peking speciality is hot-sour soup (酸辣湯), a peppery bracer of shredded pork and bamboo shoots, bean curd, spring onion and mushrooms. Wheat, not rice, is the staple in northern China. Peking restaurants serve noodles and various kinds of bread. They also work wonders with dumplings, stuffed with meat or vegetables and prepared by steaming or frying.

Shanghai. Both Peking and Shanghai restaurants serve a clever and delicious dish. "Beggar's Chicken" (貴化雞). According to legend, the inventor was a tramp who stole a chicken but had no way to cook it. Tossing in some salt and onion, he smeared the bird in mud, then roasted it in his fire. When the mud was baked dry he smashed the coating. The feathers came off with the clay and all the juicy tenderness of the bird remained. The recipe has become more sophisticated with mushrooms, pickled cabbage, shredded pork, bamboo shoots and wine in the stuffing. The ceremony of cracking the clay to reveal the chicken (nowadays wrapped in lotus leaves) adds to the sense of occasion.

In general, Shanghai food is more complicated and more thoroughly cooked than, say, Cantonese. Chilli peppers, garlic and ginger are used, though in moderation. Shanghai diners usually prefer noodles to rice.

Szechwan (or Sichuan). This food from southern China produces such sharp, hot flavours that it takes your breath away, but then awakens your palate's perceptions. Once the fiery shock of the garlicized peppers has subsided, you can distinguish many elements in unlikely coexistence—bitter, sweet, fruity, tart and sour.

Smoked duck, Szechwan style (薰鴨) is marinated in rice wine, with ginger and an array of spices, then steamed before being smoked over a specially composed wood fire.

Deep fried beef with vegetables (干燒牛肉絲) is a dish where the meat and most other ingredients—carrots, celery, peppers, garlic—are shredded and slowly fried over a low flame.

All Chinese foods aim to please the eye as well as the palate. Some Szechwan foods are also designed to appeal to the ear. "Thunder" dishes are topped with crisp rice, which sizzles and pops on meeting the other ingredients.

Tea technicalities

The Chinese virtually revere tea. They have been drinking it for centuries as a thirst-quencher, general reviver and ceremonial beverage. Jasmine-scented green tea or fermented black tea are most often encountered in Hong Kong.

Though it may take some getting used to, all the tea in China is drunk without sugar. You have no choice, so make the effort to learn to appreciate the orthodox taste. (The only exception is in some breakfast places where English tea is served with milk and sugar.)

Other drinks

The Chinese having a dinner party at the next table are probably drinking French cognac along with their meal. Hong Kong claims the world's highest per-capita consumption of brandy, possibly due to a vague belief that it has aphrodisiac qualities. European and Australian table wines are also available at prices ranging from the tolerable to the shocking.

As for Chinese wines, which have a 4,000-year history, few foreigners develop the taste. Some are too sweet, others too strong. Unlike the Chinese grape and rice wines, the wheat wines are notorious for their alcoholic power. *Mou Tai* is a breathtaking case in point.

Visiting beer-lovers have plenty of choice. The locally brewed *San Miguel* is cheap and refreshing. *Tsingtao* beer from China, in big green bottles, has a hearty European taste. You'll also find some of the best beers of Asia and Europe on better menus.

Familiar soft drinks and delicious tropical fruit juices round off the beverage list. Coffee exists, but mostly in western-style restaurants and snack bars.

Among the delights of Hong Kong: food stalls on every corner, and bounty of the South China Sea.

Other foods

While you're in the neighbourhood, take the opportunity to get to know some other Asian cuisines. Hong Kong restaurants cover all the main cooking styles of the region—Indian, Indonesian, Japanese, Korean, Thai and Vietnamese. So if you long for a vast Indonesian

rijsttafel or authentic Japanese *sushi* or Korean *kimchee*—or even "*33*" beer imported from Ho Chi Minh City—everything is possible in the restaurants of Hong Kong.

If you're not keen on oriental food, you still won't starve in Hong Kong, with its many American, British and European-style restaurants. Considering how far the food has to come, some of it is remarkably good. Ever more popular with the locals are "fast food" outlets, where you can take away a hamburger in a bag.

Several good vegetarian restaurants do creditable versions of Chinese food. A lot of locals, not just Buddhist monks, keep the places crowded.

Etiquette

Except for formal banquets the Chinese pay little attention to protocol; they slurp the soup and let bits of food drop on to the tablecloth. All the more reason not to feel self-conscious about your chopstick technique. (But never place your chopsticks across the rice bowl; let them rest on the holder provided or against a plate.)

Table napkins are not normally provided in a Chinese restaurant, but hot damp face towels are distributed at the beginning or end or both.

If a Chinese host invites you to a restaurant, put yourself in his hands; he will try to order according to his impression of your tastes. You must eat some of every dish to avoid giving offence. If you're invited to dine at a Chinese home it is the highest honour. Be sure to bring a small gift.

To Help You Order...

Have you a table?
I'd like a/an/some...

The bill, please.

Yau mo toi ah?
Ngor seung yiu...

Mai dan, m goi.

beer	**bei jau**	meat	**yuk**
chopsticks	**fai ji**	menu	**chan pye**
cup	**bui**	rice	**faan**
dessert	**tim bun**	soup	**tong**
fish	**yue**	tea	**cha**
fruit	**sang gwo**	water	**sui**
glass	**bor lay bui**	wine	**jau**

...and Read the Menu

蟹肉荳腐羹	bean curd and crabmeat soup
麻婆荳腐	bean curd with pork in pepper sauce
合桃鷄丁	diced chicken with walnuts
腰果肉丁	diced pork with cashew nuts
干燒冬筍	fried bamboo shoots and cabbage
炒鱔糊	fried eel with soya sauce
清炒蝦仁	fried shrimps
青椒肉絲	fried sliced pork with green pepper
菜扒鮮菇	mushrooms with vegetables
辣子鷄丁	shredded chicken with green pepper
豉椒牛肉	sliced beef with green pepper and bean sauce
三絲湯	sliced chicken, abalone and prawn soup
紅燒魚片	sliced fish with brown sauce
糟溜黃魚	stewed yellow fish
咕嚕肉	sweet and sour pork
鷄油津白	Tientsin cabbage and asparagus

BLUEPRINT for a Perfect Trip

How to Get There

The following information is subject to change, so consult a reliable travel agent when planning your holiday in Hong Kong.

From the United Kingdom

BY AIR: There are several daily flights from London to Hong Kong, the majority stopping at different cities en route. Passengers from Scotland and Ireland connect with flights from London. Main types of fares: first class, club (business) class, economy class, excursion fare, APEX and IPEX (Instant Purchase Excursion) fares. Flight time London–Hong Kong: 15–16 hours.

Package tours: There is a wide range of package tours available to Hong Kong with possibilities of touring in China. Most airlines offer discounts in certain Hong Kong hotels; discounts are also available on city tours.

BY SEA: There is no regular passenger ship between the U.K. and Hong Kong. Once or twice a year, there are round-the-world cruises leaving Europe and stopping at Hong Kong. Inquire at travel agents.

From North America

BY AIR: Scheduled flights link Hong Kong with various U.S. cities, some direct, but most with a stopover in one or two cities (Los Angeles/Seattle/Vancouver/Honolulu/Tokyo). As well as first, business and economy class, there are many types of fares available between North America and Hong Kong. Prices may depend on the airline, the length of stay, the dates of travel, the date of the reservation and the place of departure. Consult an informed travel agent well before departure. Flight time from Los Angeles to Hong Kong is approximately 17 hours, from New York, 22 hours.

Package tours: There are numerous GIT (Group Inclusive Tour) programmes for 3 to 7 days in Hong Kong and other cities in the Far East. Tour features include air transport, hotel accommodation, some or all meals, ground transport, and the services of a tour guide. These GITs may be extended by four days (but not to exceed a total of 35 days) to include trips to several cities in Asia.

There are also cruise tours with stops in Tokyo, Hong Kong and Singapore. Or take a 9-day or 14-day cruise from Singapore to Bali, then a flight home from Hong Kong.

When to Go

The best season to visit Hong Kong is autumn when the temperature and humidity drop and days are clear and sunny. From December until February you'll find the air moderately cold with the humidity still low; an overcoat may be necessary. In spring the humidity and temperature start rising and from May to mid-September it's hot and wet with three-quarters of the annual rainfall recorded during these months.

The following chart will give you an idea of the average monthly temperatures in Hong Kong, and the number of rainy days per month:

		J	F	M	A	M	J	J	A	S	O	N	D
Temperature	°C	15	15	18	22	25	28	28	28	27	25	21	17
	°F	59	59	64	72	77	82	82	82	81	77	70	63
Days of rain		6	8	11	12	16	21	19	17	14	8	6	5

Planning Your Budget

To give you an idea of what to expect, here are some average prices in Hong Kong dollars. However, they must be regarded as *approximate;* inflation is a factor in Hong Kong as elsewhere.

Airport. "Airbus" to Tsim Sha Tsui HK$5, to Hong Kong island (Central or Causeway Bay) HK$7. Taxi to Kowloon HK$20, to Hong Kong island HK$44–$55. Airport departure tax HK$120 for adults HK$60 for children aged 2 to 11.

Buses and trams. Buses HK$1–$7, trams HK60c, minibuses HK$1–$5, Peak Tram HK$6 for adults, HK$2 for children.

Car hire. Japanese-made cars HK$300–$450 per day, HK$1,750–$2,500 per week, collision damage waiver HK$45 per day.

Cigarettes. HK$9.50 for a packet of 20, cigars HK$25–$150.

Cinema. HK$25–$30 (no reduction for children).

Discotheque. Minimum charge (including 2 drinks), weekdays HK$70, weekends/holidays HK$90.

Ferries. *Star Ferry* HK50c–70c. *Macau:* ferry HK$23–$150, high-speed ferry HK$35–$55, hoverferry HK$45–$56, hydrofoil HK$46–$58, jetfoil HK$57–$88; add HK$15 departure tax. *Other islands* HK$4–$12. *Guangzhou* (Canton): hovercraft HK$260 return (fares to Guangzhou increase during peak seasons such as Chinese New Year).

Hairdressers. *Woman's* haircut HK$80–$170, shampoo and blow-dry HK$100–$150, permanent wave HK$200–$600.

Hotels. Hostels and guesthouses HK$160–$380, medium hotel HK$380–$890, luxury hotel HK$980 and up. Add 10% service charge and 5% government tax.

Mass Transit Railway (single fare). Adults HK$2–$5.50, children HK$1–$1.50 on weekdays, HK$1.50–$2 on Sundays and holidays.

Meals and drinks. Set lunch HK$80–$160, dinner HK$150–$300, beer or soft drink HK$10–$15, carafe of wine HK$35 and up, spirits HK$25 and up.

Medical care. HK$80–$150 for a consultation.

Taxis. HK$5 for first 2 km., HK70c for each succeeding 250 metres, HK$20 for crossing harbour tunnel.

Trains. Kowloon to Lo Wu, first class HK$32, ordinary class HK$16.

Walla wallas. HK$60–$150 per trip within the harbour, or HK$100 per hour.

An A–Z Summary
of Practical Information and Facts

A star (*) following an entry indicates that relevant prices are to be found on page 106.

AIRPORT.* Kai Tak airport, one of Asia's busiest, has a prize location almost in the centre of the city—which makes for dramatic landings amidst the rooftops of Kowloon. The single runway projects into the harbour on reclaimed land.

A

Arrival: Arriving passengers go through immigration and customs checks in modern, efficient surroundings. Beyond the baggage inspection area you will find a bank, a hotel-reservation desk and an information office of the Hong Kong Tourist Association.

There are several ways of getting into town. Major hotels operate their own limousine service for guests; look for the dispatcher at the sign identifying your hotel. (Most hotels add the fare to your account.) Alternatively you can take a taxi. You should be charged only what the meter reads—plus an additional fixed sum if you take the tunnel to Hong Kong island. Don't forget that the taxi meter is registering Hong Kong—not U.S.—dollars.

Airport coaches link Kai Tak with the principal hotel zones. "Airbus" A1 goes to the district of Tsim Sha Tsui, A2 to Hong Kong Central and A3 to Causeway Bay. Wherever you're heading, it's only a few miles from the airport—though heavy traffic can make it seem much longer.

Departure: Airport coaches pass by main hotels every 15 minutes but limousines will come only if previously arranged by the hotel hall porter. Taxis might be difficult to find at rush hour. The Hong Kong Tourist Association warns that in heavy traffic congestion, it can take up to an hour and a half to reach the airport from central Hong Kong and 45 minutes from Kowloon's hotel district.

Check-in time is one hour before the flight's listed departure. After that you'll be free to use the duty-free shop, as well as all the usual facilities of a major international airport. A departure tax is levied, payable in Hong Kong dollars only.

Tipping note: While it is officially not obligatory to tip an airport porter, in practice HK$3–4 per bag is expected.

B **BABY-SITTING.** The first-class hotels can arrange for an English-speaking baby-sitter quite easily. Or you can look in the Yellow Pages for an agency. Baby-sitting services are not highly developed in Hong Kong; most well-to-do residents have *amahs* (maids), and many Chinese families take the children along when they go out.

BUSES and TRAMS.* Bus service is good and inexpensive, though uncomfortably crowded at peak hours. If you plan to do much sightseeing by bus, buy the timetable books issued by the Hong Kong island operator, China Motor Bus. Most bus stops are marked by a disc saying "all buses stop here". On most buses you must deposit the exact fare into the box next to the driver as you enter.

Trams: Hong Kong's colourful double-deck trams are a pleasant way to see the sights and an efficient means of travelling short distances. Slow but sure, they traverse the north coast of Hong Kong island between Kennedy Town and Shau Kei Wan.

You enter through the rear doors, fitted with turnstiles. The exit is at the front, and you pay as you leave, dropping the exact amount into the fare box. It's a flat rate regardless of the distance travelled.

| Where's the bus stop? | **Bar zee tsam hai bean doe?** |
| Where's the tram stop? | **Deen che tsam hai bean doe?** |

C **CAR HIRE.*** International and local car rental agencies operate in Hong Kong with both drive-yourself and chauffeur-driven cars. They offer Japanese, European and American models.

Major credit cards are accepted by many agencies; a deposit is asked for only if you pay cash. The minimum age required is 25 and you must have held a driving licence for at least two years.

In view of the problems of traffic and parking, most tourists stick to taxis and public transport.

CIGARETTES, CIGARS, TOBACCO.* American, European and Asian brands of cigarettes are sold all over Hong Kong at prices most tourists would consider bargains. Certain tobacconists sell a wide range of cigars and pipe tobaccos. Smoking is a widespread habit in Hong Kong; restrictions against smoking in public places are not severe.

| A packet of cigarettes, please. | **M goi nay, yat bau yeen tsai.** |
| filter-tipped/without filter | **lui tchui/mo lui tchui** |

CLOTHING. From May to September very lightweight clothing is called for, though a raincoat might come in handy. Inside restaurants and hotels, beware of the air-conditioning, which can be freezing; have a cardigan or shawl just in case. In winter—from late December to February—warm suits and dresses are necessary and you may even see the occasional fur coat.

Informality is generally the rule, though women often wear long dresses and skirts. Better restaurants and nightclubs expect men to wear jacket and tie. For sightseeing and shopping, virtually any fashion is appropriate, except that shorts are out of place in business districts and perhaps certain Chinese temples.

Bring along comfortable low-heeled shoes, as walking up and down steep slopes is unavoidable in Hong Kong.

COMMUNICATIONS

Post Offices. As in the United States, the post office of Hong Kong deals only with parcels and letters. The local postal service is fast and efficient; all postmen can read both Chinese and English addresses. Airmail deliveries are speedy, but packages sent surface mail may take six to ten weeks on the way to Europe or North America.

Stamps are sold at post offices and hotels. Post boxes are red pillar boxes, as in Britain. For opening hours see under HOURS.

Telegrams: Cable and Wireless Limited runs Hong Kong's telecommunications links with the rest of the world. Hotels normally send telegrams for their clients, or you can go to the C&W office at Exchange Square Tower 1, Hong Kong, which is open to the public 24 hours a day.

Telephones: Hong Kong's telephone system for both local and international calls is excellent. You will find few phone booths or coin-operated telephones; if you do, they require a HK$1 coin. Most people simply pick up any telephone—in a bar or shop—and use it even without asking permission. Local calls cost the subscriber nothing in Hong Kong, hence the generosity of phone owners.

Phones ring according to the British system. A terse low-pitched ring-ring, ring-ring means the number you want is ringing. If the line is engaged, a high-pitched interrupted tone sounds. A high continuous hum means the number you want is out of order.

For information (directory enquiries) dial 108; if you have difficulties in getting a number, dial 109. For overseas calls dial 100 or go to a Cable and Wireless office.

C COMPLAINTS. The Hong Kong Tourist Association will mediate between visitors and shops and establishments which belong to the association. In cases of overcharging by taxi drivers, complaints should be addressed to the police. In other cases, complaints may be directed to one of the following:

The Consumer Council, 3rd floor Asian House, 1 Hennessy Road, Wanchai, Hong Kong. Tel. (5) 20 05 11.

The Community Advice Bureau, St. John's Cathedral, Garden Road, Hong Kong. Tel. (5) 24 54 44.

CONSULATES. For complete lists of consulates, look in the classified directory (Yellow Pages) for Hong Kong island—under *Consulates* or, for Commonwealth countries, under *Commissioners*. In case of Hong Kong visa problems, consult the

Hong Kong Immigration Department, Mirror Tower, 61 Mody Road, Tsim Sha Tsui East, Kowloon. Tel. (3) 7 33 31 11.

Australia: 23rd–24th floors, Harbour Centre, 25 Harbour Rd., Hong Kong. Tel. (5) 73 18 81.

Canada: 10th–14th floors, Tower 1, Exchange Square, Hong Kong. Tel. (5) 8 10 43 21.

Eire: 8th floor, Prince's Building, Hong Kong. Tel. (5) 22 60 22.

New Zealand: Connaught Centre, 34th floor, Connaught Rd. Central, Hong Kong. Tel. (5) 22 51 20.

South Africa: 27th floor, Sunning Plaza, 10 Hysan Ave., Causeway Bay, Hong Kong. Tel. (5) 17 32 79.

U.S.A.: 26 Garden Rd., Hong Kong. Tel. (5) 23 90 11.

For consulate office hours see under HOURS.

CONVERTER CHARTS. Hong Kong is going metric, but many Imperial and Chinese measures are still in daily use.

Chinese measures are common in the markets and at the drapers', chemists' and jewellers' frequented by the locals. Food products are generally sold by the *catty*. Other items are measured by the *tael* (e.g. gold), *fun* and *chin*. Western-style supermarkets and groceries use all sorts of weights and measures depending on where the merchandise comes from.

The charts given below will help you make conversions in the Chinese, Imperial and metric systems. For fluid and distance measures, see p. 112.

Length

1 tsün	=	1.5 in.	=	37 mm.
1 chek	=	1.2 ft.	=	37 cm.

Weight

1 leung (tael)	=	1.3 oz	=	38 g
1 kan (catty)	=	1.3 lbs	=	600 g
1 tam (picul)	=	133 lbs	=	60 kg

Length

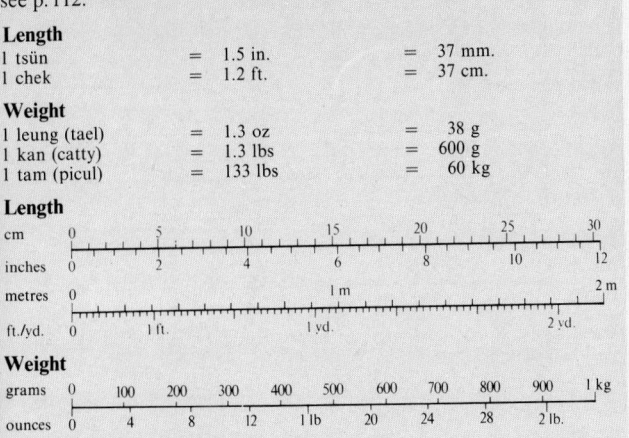

Weight

(All figures are approximate.)

CRIME and THEFT. As the signs in the trams warn you, "Beware of pickpockets". This applies to any crowded place, and Hong Kong has some of the most crowded places you've ever seen. Otherwise, tourists have nothing special to fear.

DRIVING IN HONG KONG. Anyone over 18 with a valid licence can drive in Hong Kong for 12 months without having to apply for a local licence.

Driving conditions: As in Britain, Hong Kong traffic keeps to the left. Congestion is a serious problem, sometimes leading to impatient, imprudent driving. Some inept local drivers are said to have received their licences by bribing inspectors—before the government cracked down on such practices. Beware, also, of inattentive pedestrians. Speed limit: 30 miles per hour in towns, elsewhere as marked.

Parking: This can be a headache, especially in central areas, despite the new multi-storey car-parks. In busy streets the meters operate from

D 8 a.m. to midnight, Monday to Saturday… and wardens are ever-alert. Sunday and holiday parking meters are to be introduced in some districts.

Breakdowns: Telephone the firm from which you hired the car. In an emergency, dial 999 for the police.

Fluid measures

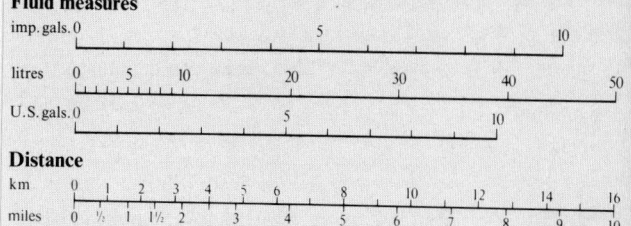

Distance

Road signs: Most road signs in Hong Kong are the standard international pictographs.

The following words may help you in explaining your problems to non-English-speaking Chinese:

There's been an accident.	**Yau yi ngoi a.**
collision	**jong che**
flat tire	**baau tai**

E **ELECTRICITY.** Standard voltage in Hong Kong is 200-volt, 50-cycle A.C. Many hotels have razor fittings for standard plugs and voltages. Elsewhere, sockets come in many sizes—the vestige of an old British tradition. American irons need special adaptors.

EMERGENCIES. Dial 999 and ask for the Police, Fire or Ambulance department.

The main hospitals treat urgent medical problems 24 hours a day in their emergency wards; hotels often have doctors on call.

Round-the-clock service for dental emergencies is found at: The Adventist Hospital, 40 Stubbs Road, Hong Kong.

The Yellow Pages of the telephone directory has listings under *Physicians and Surgeons* and *Dental Practitioners*.

Help!	**Gau meng ah!**
Police!	**Geng tsa!**

ENTRY FORMALITIES and CUSTOMS. All visitors must have a passport or other valid travel document. U.K. citizens are generally granted a three- to six-month stay without a visa. Nationals of more than 50 other countries, including the U.S.A., Canada, Australia and New Zealand, need no visas for visits of up to one month (to three months in some cases). South African nationals may stay in Hong Kong for up to seven days without a visa. For longer visits a formal application has to be made. Further information: British consulates or High Commissions. Or consult the Hong Kong Immigration Department: Mirror Tower, 61 Mody Rd., Tsim Sha Tsui East, Kowloon.

Though Hong Kong is a free port, excise duties are charged on alcohol and tobacco. Here are the quotas on items you can bring in duty-free and, when returning home, into your own country:

Into:	Cigarettes		Cigars		Tobacco	Spirits		Wine
Hong Kong	200	or	50	or	250 g.	1 l.	or	1 l.
Australia	200	or	250 g.	or	250 g.	1 l.	or	1 l.
Canada	200	and	50	and	900 g.	1.1 l.	or	1.1 l.
Eire	200	or	50	or	250 g.	1 l.	and	2 l.
N. Zealand	200	or	50	or	250 g.	1.1 l.	and	4.5 l.
S. Africa	400	and	50	and	250 g.	1 l.	and	2 l.
U.K.	200	or	50	or	250 g.	1 l.	and	2 l.
U.S.A.	200	and	100	and	*	1 l.	or	1 l.
* a reasonable quantity								

Firearms must be declared and surrendered into official custody until the visitor leaves Hong Kong. A reasonable quantity of perfume (in opened bottles) may be brought in, and there are no currency restrictions in either direction.

FERRIES and BOAT EXCURSIONS.* Hundreds of thousands of passengers cross Hong Kong harbour every day on ferryboats. The most familiar to tourists is the Star Ferry, the fastest, cheapest and most pleasant way to go between Tsim Sha Tsui (Kowloon) and central Hong Kong. The ferries operate from 6.30 a.m. to 11.30 p.m.

F   The Hongkong and Yaumati Ferry Company (HYF), called the world's largest ferryboat operator, serves various Kowloon ports as well as outlying islands. Study the timetable carefully so you can get off and explore, then catch a later ferry back. The HYF has recently started a hovercraft service between Hong Kong and Guangzhou (Canton). The journey lasts from two to three hours and tickets are obtainable from: China Travel Service, Queen's Rd. Central.

Private tourism companies run many different harbour and island excursions with guides and refreshments. Their flamboyant ferries and modified junks dock near Star Ferry (in Kowloon and Hong Kong). Some of their programmes consist of combination tram and ferry rides, often ending with a splendid Chinese meal on board. Included on such an itinerary may be a visit to the Hong Kong night market or to villages and temples on an island en route.

You can go to Macau either by jetfoil, hoverferry or hydrofoil. The journey takes about an hour. Or you may prefer the luxurious high-speed ferries. Somewhat slower than the above, but considerably faster than conventional ferry boats, they make the crossing in about 90 minutes.

See under HOURS for times when these services operate.

FUNICULAR. The Peak Tram funicular railway, more than 90 years old, links Garden Road with Victoria Peak. It climbs straight up the mountainside to the Peak Tower, where you'll be able to get a panoramic view of Hong Kong and, on clear days, China as well.

It's a popular tourist attraction and overcrowded on Sundays and holidays; operating hours are from 7 a.m. to midnight.

G   **GUIDES.** Various private companies run guided tours of Hong Kong, the New Territories and the islands. See *Sightseeing Tours* or *Travel Bureaux* in the Yellow Pages of the telephone directory; the latter classification also includes firms offering interpreters or companions.

H   **HAIRDRESSERS'.*** The top hotels have first-class hairdressing salons. Hong Kong also has several establishments run by internationally known stylists. The prices in luxury shops are several times higher than in the smaller, neighbourhood places. Men's and women's hairdressers are usually separate.

Twirling barber poles are found in every Hong Kong neighbourhood
114   or village, sometimes announcing an outdoor barber shop where clip-

ping or shearing is done in old-fashioned conditions. Visitors will appreciate these shops more for the local colour than the hair-do.

haircut	**fay fat**
shampoo and set	**sai tau, tchui fat**
blow dry (brushing)	**tchui gon**
colour rinse	**yimm fat**
Trim a bit off (here).	**Tsin siu siu (ni doe).**
Trim a little more off (here).	**Tsin dor dee (ni doe).**

HIKING. Local hikers fan out every weekend through the New Territories, the larger islands, and Hong Kong island as well, where a network of paths discloses surprisingly open and appealing scenery. Maps of hiking trails in the popular areas are available at the Government Publications Centre in the General Post Office, Hong Kong.

HOTELS. * Hong Kong has close to 20,000 hotel rooms, most of them in luxury or first-class hotels, which is bad news for the budget-conscious tourist. From time to time the influx of visitors exceeds the supply of space, mostly in October and November but occasionally in the spring as well. During these seasons advance bookings are essential.

Hong Kong hotels include some establishments known around the world for their comfort and service. Even the more modest hotels are usually air-conditioned and offer more than just the basic services. The announced rates for hotels cover the room price only; a 10 per cent service charge and a 5 per cent government tax are added to the bill at check-out time.

HOURS. Most government offices are open from 9 a.m. to 1 p.m. and 2 to 5 p.m., Monday to Friday, and on Saturday from 9 a.m. to 1 p.m.

Banks: Standard banking hours are 9.30 or 10 a.m. to 3 p.m., Monday to Friday and until noon on Saturday, but many banks open earlier and continue operating until 4.30 p.m. Money-changers' offices, found in most neighbourhoods, stay open much longer than banks. Even later you can change money at the airport or a hotel.

Consulates: Generally speaking, they're open from 9 a.m. to noon and from 2 to 5 p.m., Monday to Friday. To make absolutely sure, telephone first.

H **Ferries:** These ply very regularly and frequently, not only between Hong Kong and Kowloon, but also to the other major islands. They start at about 7 a.m. and stop often as late as midnight (the Star Ferry works between 6.30 a.m. and 11.30 p.m.).

The jetfoil and hydrofoil services to Macau start at 7.45 a.m. and stop at midnight. The Macau Ferry starts at 9 a.m. and operates until night.

The Hong Kong Guangzhou (Canton) hovercraft service has three departures daily.

Museums

Most museums are closed on public holidays like Christmas Eve, New Year's Eve, the Lunar New Year, etc.

Flagstaff House Museum of Tea Ware: 10 a.m.–5 p.m. daily except Wednesdays.

Fung Ping Shan Museum: 10 a.m.–6 p.m. daily except Thursdays and public holidays.

Hong Kong Museum of Art: 10 a.m.–6 p.m. daily except Thursdays; Sundays and public holidays 1–6 p.m.

Hong Kong Museum of History: open daily except Fridays 10 a.m.– 6 p.m.; Sundays and public holidays 1–6 p.m.

Hong Kong Space Museum: sky show in Space Theatre Mondays and Wednesdays to Saturdays at 2.30, 4, 5.30, 7.30 and 9 p.m., Sundays and public holidays at 11 a.m. and 12.30 p.m. Shows in English at 9 p.m. on Sundays and Wednesdays, at 4 p.m. on Mondays and Fridays. Session in Exhibition Hall and Hall of Solar Sciences Mondays and Wednesdays to Saturdays from 2 to 10 p.m., Sundays and public holidays from 10.30 a.m. to 10 p.m.

Lei Cheng Uk Museum: 10 a.m.–1 p.m. and 2–6 p.m. daily except Thursdays; Sundays and public holidays 1–6 p.m.

Museu Luís de Camões, Macau: 11 a.m.–5 p.m. daily except Wednesdays and public holidays.

Museum of Chinese Historical Relics: 10 a.m.–6 p.m. daily.

Sung Dynasty Village (Wax Museum): 11 a.m.–9 p.m. daily.

Post offices: Convenient post offices are found in Hong Kong Central and in Kowloon, open from 8 a.m. to 6 p.m., Monday to Saturday. Elsewhere they're open during the same hours from Monday to Friday, and from 9 a.m. to 1 p.m. on Saturday.

Shops: Major shops in Hong Kong are open from 9 or 10 a.m. to 6 or 7 p.m. daily except Sunday. But in Kowloon and Causeway Bay, for instance, shopping continues until 9.30 or 10 p.m., Sunday included.

LANGUAGE. The official languages of Hong Kong are English and Chinese; Cantonese is commonly spoken by the local residents. (Though Chinese dialects may vary from one another considerably in pronunciation, the written language is the same.) For practical purposes English is understood in most situations.

The following approximations of Cantonese greetings may help you make contact with the locals:

Good morning	**jo san**	Thank you	**m goi**
Good afternoon	**ng on***	(for service)	
Good evening	**mang on**	Please (invitation)	**tcheng**
Good night	**jo tau**	Please (for service)	**m goi**
Thank you (for a gift)	**dor jeh**	Goodbye	**joy geen**

* The Cantonese commonly use a more complicated expression meaning, "Have you eaten yet?" The reply is either. "Yes, I've eaten, thank you", or "No, not yet".

Here are some everyday Hong Kong words:

amah	housemaid
chop	seal or stamp on a document
coolie	cargo-carrying labourer
fung shui	lucky siting of building or graves
gwailo	"foreign devil"
hong	big business firm
joss	luck
pak pai	illegal taxi
schroff	cashier
yam seng	"cheers", "bottoms up"

LAUNDRY and DRY-CLEANING. In many hotels laundry and dry-cleaning are routinely returned the same day. Of course, prices are much higher than in neighbourhood establishments. For addresses off the tourist track, look in the Yellow Pages of the telephone directory under *Cleaners and Dyers.* Hong Kong also has a number of launderettes, where you can wash, spin and dry your own load of clothing for a moderate price. Look in the Yellow Pages under *Launderers—self service.*

LOST and FOUND PROPERTY. Check first with your hotel receptionist if you lose anything, then report the loss to the nearest police station or "reporting centre", a sub-station where the police maintain contact with the public in busy areas.

MAPS. The Hong Kong Tourist Association has free maps covering the principal commercial areas of Hong Kong and Kowloon. They also sell various other maps and street directories, as do leading bookstores. Maps meeting almost any need are sold at the Government Publications Centre in the General Post Office, Hong Kong.

MASS TRANSIT RAILWAY. The fast, cheerful, air-conditioned trains of the underground railway system link the central district of Hong Kong with Kowloon and the New Territories. An Island Line runs along the northern coast of Hong Kong island. Maps in MTR stations and in every carriage depict the routes; announcements in Cantonese and English identify the stops. Tickets are issued, inspected and finally collected by machines, but humans are available in the stations to make change and give advice.

MEDICAL CARE.* See also EMERGENCIES. Since health care can be expensive, consult your insurance company at home for advice about a policy covering illness or accident on holiday.

Requirements for vaccinations change from time to time so be sure to check with your travel agent or airline before departure. At last report Hong Kong had dispensed with the requirement for smallpox or cholera vaccination, except for passengers arriving from infected areas. Macau normally follows suit.

Malaria has made a comeback in recent years in south-east Asia. Fansidar, a drug available without prescription in Hong Kong, is an effective safeguard against the mosquito-borne disease.

Hong Kong has up-to-date hospitals on both sides of the harbour. For minor ailments, chemists can often recommend and supply certain medicines, but you won't be able to get a foreign prescription filled.

Many local pharmacies adhere to both western and eastern concepts of health care, displaying familiar pills and bottles along with exotic herbs, roots, dried seahorses and powdered antlers.

I want to see a…	**Ngor yiu tai…**
doctor	**yee sang**
dentist	**nga yee**

MEETING PEOPLE. In the rush and hubbub of Hong Kong a smile goes a long way. But don't be disappointed if the reaction seems cool. The Chinese are not demonstrative and may be flustered by those who are. As in most other countries, you can usually meet new friends by striking up a conversation in a bar or pub. In the fleshpots of Wanchai or Tsim Sha Tsui, the amity is professional, rentable by the drink.

MINIBUSES. Hong Kong's "public light buses", seating 14 passengers, are fast and convenient. You can hail them everywhere and get off almost anywhere along their route. The destination is lit up atop the front window in Chinese only on most buses, and in English as well on some others. Occasionally the fare is shown in Chinese numerals only. Pay the driver as you leave and keep a sufficient number of coins in your pocket, as it's not easy to get change.

Minibuses marked with a green stripe go to the Mid Levels, up to the Peak and Aberdeen. You can find them in Central. Minibuses marked with a red stripe have routes around West Point, Central, Causeway Bay, Quarry Bay and Chai Wan. Some of them also go over to Kowloon and can be hailed in Causeway Bay or Wanchai.

MONEY MATTERS

Currency: Hong Kong's freely convertible currency, the Hong Kong dollar (abbreviated $ or HK$), is divided into 100 cents (abbreviated c). Banknotes are circulated in denominations of 10, 50, 100, 500 and 1,000 dollars. They are issued by two local banks, not by the Hong Kong government, which does, however, mint the coins. They come in denominations of 5, 10, 20 and 50 cents and 1, 2 and 5 dollars. Note that the 10-cent and 50-cent pieces look confusingly alike.

Traveller's cheques: Traveller's cheques are widely accepted in shops, though you'll probably get a better exchange rate at a bank. You must show your passport when you cash a cheque.

Credit cards: Major hotels, restaurants and shops accept the well-known charge cards. Even the big stores owned by Communist China recognize certain credit cards.

If you plan to make a large foreign currency transaction it's worthwhile to shop around, as exchange rates vary from place to place and day to day. Both foreign and local banks have branches all over the territory, including small towns. For banking hours see under HOURS.

NEWSPAPERS and MAGAZINES. Hong Kong has more than 100 newspapers in the Chinese language. The two most popular English language dailies are the *South China Morning Post* and the *Hong Kong*

Standard. The *Asian Wall Street Journal,* published Monday to Friday in Hong Kong, emphasizes business and financial coverage. The *International Herald Tribune,* edited in Paris, is printed simultaneously in Hong Kong six days a week. Newspapers and magazines from Europe, Asia and the United States are sold at hotel bookstalls and leading bookshops.

PHOTOGRAPHY. Hong Kong is a good place to buy duty-free camera equipment, and to use it. Film is not expensive; the processing is fast and reasonably priced. But cine-film takes longer, as it may be sent to Australia for development.

At Kai Tak airport the luggage of departing passengers is X-rayed for security reasons. The best way of protecting your films is to keep them in your hand luggage and remove them just before the inspection.

POLICE. The Royal Hong Kong Police Force is one of the world's best equipped, with computerized and radio-controlled forces. It deals with crime, traffic and even coastguard duties. Living up to Hong Kong's reputation as a fashion centre, the police dress in natty, trimly tailored uniforms. Constables with red shoulder badges are considered fluent in English, but all police are to some extent bilingual.

Where's the police station, please? **Tsai goon hai bean doe, m goi?**

PRICES. For an idea of what things cost, see the section Planning Your Budget on page 106. Except for Chinese food, few big bargains brighten daily life in Hong Kong. Housing, to give an extreme example, is more expensive than almost anywhere in the world. For the tourist, though, shopping is one of the great attractions, and real bargains can still be found in cameras and hi-fi equipment, jewellery, some tailoring and products from across the border in China.

PUBLIC HOLIDAYS. Thanks to the convergence of British and Chinese traditions, Hong Kong celebrates 17 holidays a year. Though the banks close, most businesses carry on as usual. The only holiday on which Hong Kong really shuts down is the Lunar New Year. Chinese holidays are fixed according to the lunar calendar, so exact dates cannot always be given.

New Year's Day	January 1
Lunar New Year (3–4 days)	January or February
Ching Ming Festival	April
Good Friday	March or April
The day following Good Friday	
Easter Monday	
The Queen's Birthday	June
Tuen Ng (Dragon Boat) Festival	May or June
The first weekday in July	
The first Monday in August	
Liberation Day	Last Monday in August
The day following the mid-Autumn Festival	September or October
Chung Yeung Festival	October
Christmas Day	December 25
Boxing Day	December 26

RADIO and TV. Hong Kong has two TV channels in English and two in Chinese. The Chinese channels sometimes show foreign-language films in the original version with Chinese subtitles.

The official Radio Television Hong Kong (RTHK) broadcasts three English radio services. RTHK 3 and 4 carry several BBC newscasts every day. RTHK 5 relays BBC World Service programming at night.

Commercial Radio Hong Kong operates one English station.

RELIGIOUS SERVICES. Confucianism, Buddhism and Taoism are the major religions in Hong Kong. The territory, however, also has hundreds of Christian churches and chapels, the oldest being St. John's Cathedral (Church of England), built in the first decade of British rule. For details of services consult the telephone book's Yellow Pages under *Church Organizations.* The Saturday issue of the *South China Morning Post* runs announcements from churches.

Hong Kong also has Hindu, Jewish and Moslem houses of worship.

RICKSHAWS. On a small scale they continue as a Hong Kong tourist attraction, at least until the remaining rickshaw men retire; no new licences are issued. Fares must be agreed on before a trip. Nowadays most tourists are content to be photographed in the conveyance without actually going anywhere, but this, too, requires a payment.

T **TAXIS.*** Hong Kong's metered taxis (with white TAXI signs on the roofs) are relatively inexpensive. The law does not compel a driver to stop when hailed, even if his "for hire" flag is showing. But once you have successfully stopped a taxi and taken a seat, you have the legal right to be taken wherever you say. If the driver demurs, or attempts to overcharge you, complain to the nearest police constable or traffic warden.

Many drivers have only a limited knowledge of English. A further problem: places with English names normally have totally different ones in Chinese. So it might be useful to have someone write your destination on a piece of paper in Chinese characters. Or you can point to the location, using the maps in this book, or our glossary of Hong Kong place names (see page 19).

Tipping is not obligatory but it's customary to add about 10 per cent to the charge on the meter.

TIME DIFFERENCES. Before you make any overseas telephone calls, have a look at the chart, lest you wake someone halfway round the world:

New York	London	**Hong Kong**	Sydney
7 a.m.	noon	**7 p.m.**	9 p.m.

The above hours refer to the period March/April—September/October, when many countries in the northern hemisphere move their clocks one hour ahead (Daylight Saving Time). Hong Kong stays the same year-round, at GMT + 8.

TIPPING. In Hong Kong's service-oriented society, tips are definitely part of everyday life. Even in restaurants, where a service charge is usually added to the bill, an additional tip is expected.

Some suggestions:

Hairdresser/Barber	10–20%
Lavatory attendant	HK$ 1–2
Maid, per week	HK$ 50
Hotel porter, per bag	HK$ 3–5

Taxi driver	10% (optional)
Tourist guide	10% (optional)
Waiter	5–10%

TOILETS. Public conveniences are fairly easy to find but not necessarily very nice. If you have a choice, go into a hotel. When the lavatory of a hotel or restaurant is attended, a tip is appropriate.

Where are the toilets?   **Chi saw hai bean doe?**

TOURIST INFORMATION OFFICES. The Hong Kong Tourist Association operates information and gift centres at key areas for visitors, starting in the arrival hall at Kai Tak airport. Leaflets and maps—and answers to questions—may also be obtained at the information and gift centre on the Star Ferry concourse in Kowloon (open seven days a week). The head office is at:

35th floor, Connaught Centre, Connaught Rd. Central, Hong Kong.

A telephone information service for visitors is available from 8 a.m. to 6 p.m. Monday to Friday and from 8 a.m. to 1 p.m. on Saturdays and Sundays. Dial (3) 7 22 55 55.

Addresses of some overseas offices of the Hong Kong Tourist Association:

Australia and New Zealand: National Australia Bank House, 20th floor, 255 George St., Sydney, N.S.W. 2000. Tel. (02) 251-2855.

United Kingdom: 125 Pall Mall, London SW1Y 5EA. Tel. (01) 930-4775.

U.S.A.: Suite 2323, 333 North Michigan Ave., Chicago, IL 60601-3966. Tel. (312) 782-1960.
548 Fifth Ave., New York, NY 10036-5092. Tel. (212) 869-5008/9.
Suite 200, 421 Powell St., San Francisco, CA 94102-1568. Tel. (416) 781-4582.

TRAINS.* The Kowloon–Canton Railway carries freight (mostly food) from China to Hong Kong and commuters between Kowloon and the New Territories. The Hong Kong section of the line is 21 miles long, to the border town of Lo Wu.

Generally trains leave the new Kowloon terminal at Hung Hom at least once an hour from 5.30 a.m. to 10.30 p.m.

W   **WALLA WALLAS.** The local name (sometimes spelled *wallah wallah*) for small motorboats working as water taxis. Before the construction of the harbour tunnel they were a popular way of crossing between Kowloon and Hong Kong after the ferries shut down at night. Still available, though, at Queen's Pier, Hong Kong, and near Star Ferry, Kowloon, they're especially handy for sailors who've missed the boat.

WATER. Hong Kong tap water is officially qualified as safe to drink, but most local people prefer to boil it first. Purified ice-water is provided in many hotel rooms and western-style restaurants. In Chinese restaurants the usual thirst-quencher is hot tea.

a bottle of drinking water	**yat tchun sui**
iced water	**dung sui**

Y   **YOUTH HOSTELS.** Hong Kong's six youth hostels are located in remote scenic areas, too far from the bright lights to serve as a base for most foreign tourists, but fine for hiking trips to get away from the city rush.

Information: Youth Hostels Association. Tel. (5) 700985.

For central accommodation there are four hotel-style establishments of the YMCA and YWCA, one of them next door to the ultra-luxurious Peninsula Hotel, Kowloon. Considerably cheaper accommodation may be found in hostels and guest houses around town. For information, consult the Student Travel Bureau:

Room 1021, Star House, Kowloon. Tel. (3) 7213169.

NUMBERS

1	**yat**	6	**luk**
2	**yee**	7	**tchat**
3	**sam**	8	**baat**
4	**say**	9	**gau**
5	**ng**	10	**sub**

SIGNS OF HONG KONG

上車	ENTRANCE (bus or tram)
落車	EXIT (bus or tram)
請勿吸煙	NO SMOKING
兩	TAEL
斤	CATTY
警察	POLICE
男厠	MEN'S TOILET
女厠	WOMEN'S TOILET
危險	DANGER
食水	DRINKABLE (water)
不可飲用	NOT DRINKABLE
休息	CLOSED (office or shop)

SOME USEFUL EXPRESSIONS

yes/no	**hai/mm hai**
excuse me	**doi mm jue**
where/when/how	**bean doe/gay sze/dim yeung**
how long/how far	**gay noi/gay yuen**
today/tomorrow	**gum yat/ting yat**
day/week/month/year	**yat/sing kay/yuet/leen**
left/right	**jaw/yau**
up/down	**seung/har**
good/bad	**ho/wai**
big/small	**dai/sai**
cheap/expensive	**peng/guai**
hot/cold	**yeet/dung**
old/new	**gau/sun**
open/closed	**hoi/kwan**
Does anyone here speak English?	**Bin gor sik gong ying mun?**
I don't understand.	**Ngor mm ming pa.**
Please write it down.	**Ching seh dai.**
What time is it?	**Gay dim chung?**
I'd like...	**Ngor yiu...**
How much is that?	**Gay doe cheen?**

125

Index

An asterisk (*) next to a page number indicates a map reference. For index to Practical Information, see inside front cover.

INDEX